DEPARTMENT OF SOCIAL SECURITY

RESEARCH REPORT No 57

HELPING DISABLED WORKERS

Disability Working Allowance
and Supported Employment

Gerry Zarb, Nigel Jackson and Phil Taylor

A report of research carried out by the Policy Studies Institute
on behalf of the Department of Social Security

London: The Stationery Office

First published 1996

ISBN 0 11 762440 3
ISSN 0961 5695

Views expressed in this report are not necessarily those of the Department or any other government department.

Standing Order Service

Are you making full use of The Stationery Office's Standing Order Service?

The Standing Order Service is a free monitoring of the publications of your choice from over 4,000 classifications in 30 major subject areas. We send you your books as they are published along with an invoice.

The benefits to you are:

● automatic supply of your choice of classification on publication

● no need for time consuming and costly research, telephone calls and scanning of daily publication lists

● saving on the need and the costs of placing individual orders

We can supply a wide range of publications on standing order, from individual annual publications to all publication on a selected subject. If you do not already use this free service, or think you are not using it to its full capability, why not contact us and discuss your requirements?

You can contact us at:

The Stationery Office
Standing Order Department
PO Box 276
London SW8 5DT,

Tel 0171 873 8466; *fax* 0171 873 8222

We look forward to hearing from you.

CONTENTS

ACKNOWLEDGMENTS

Several people were involved in assisting with this research. At the Department of Social Security, Peter Craig and Kirby Swales were responsible for managing the project and made valuable comments on the various findings and drafts as the research progressed. The Association for Supported Employment (formerly known as the Association of Supported Employment Agencies), the Employment Service and Remploy all helped with providing background information as well as the information required to compile the samples for the research. At the Policy Studies Institute, Richard Berthoud and Karen Rowlingson both contributed to the design of the study and provided helpful comments at various stages of the research. Finally, special thanks are due to the staff and employees in the sheltered workshops and Supported Employment Agencies who gave up their time to take part in the research.

LIST OF ABBREVIATIONS

AfSE	Association for Supported Employment
ASEA	Association of Supported Employment Agencies
ATC	Adult Training Centre
BEL	Benefit Enquiry Line
CAA	Constant Attendance Allowance
CAB/x	Citzens' Advice Bureau/x
DEA	Disability Employment Adviser
DLA	Disability Living Allowance
DSS	Department of Social Security
DWA	Disability Working Allowance
ES	Employment Service
IB	Incapacity Benefit
ISdp	Income Support with a disability premium or higher pension premium
IVB	Invalidity Benefit
PACT	Placement, Assessment and Counselling Team
PSI	Policy Studies Institute
QB	Qualifying Benefit
SEA	Supported Employment Agencies
SEPACS	Sheltered Employment Procurement and Consultancy Service
SPSS	Statistical Package for the Social Sciences

EXECUTIVE SUMMARY

1 Introduction and background

- The Disability Working Allowance (DWA) was introduced in April 1992. The benefit is intended to help some disabled people move into or remain in employment.

- Take-up of DWA has been lower than forecast. The DSS commissioned this study to find out whether there are eligible non-recipients or potential recipients of DWA in supported employment and, if there are, to investigate how these people can be encouraged to claim DWA.

- Earlier research has suggested three main reasons for the low number of people receiving DWA: non-eligibility; non-take up by people who are eligible for DWA; and the low rate of transition off long-term incapacity benefits.

- The study has included an eligibility audit among a sample of disabled people working in supported employment. The audit survey has been designed to find out about their earnings, benefits and household circumstances, and to examine how many people might be eligible for DWA.

- The study has also examined the role of 'key workers' in supported employment to find out what kind of role they might have in terms of raising awareness, and encouraging take-up of, DWA.

- The main part of the research is based on eight case studies in Remploy and local authority/independent sector sheltered workshops and Supported Employment Agencies (SEAs).

2 Findings from interviews with key workers

- There are three main types of supported employment: sheltered workshops run by Remploy; sheltered workshops run by local authorities or voluntary/independent sector agencies; and SEAs.

- The key difference is between sheltered workshops (both Remploy and local authority/independent workshops) and SEAs. In the former, employees are employed by, and work in, the workshops. SEAs on the other hand, do not employ disabled people directly but seek to place them in jobs with host employers.

- There are about 23,000 employees in supported employment as a whole. Workers in supported employment have a range of impairments, but most of those in SEAs have learning difficulties.

- There is quite a wide variation in the roles that key workers perform in giving advice about benefits. In general, workers in SEAs are more prepared to give advice than those in sheltered workshops.

- Workers in SEAs tended to have more contacts with outside agencies than those in local authority/independent, and especially Remploy, workshops.

- Three main obstacles to key workers advising people about DWA were identified: the fact that some key workers, especially in sheltered workshops, do not see this as part of their role; their concerns about the possibility of giving people incorrect advice; and their lack of detailed knowledge about DWA.

- The main disadvantages to DWA were perceived as complex rules and claim forms, the 'benefits trap', the lack of understanding and information about DWA, and the anxiety around, and difficulty of, reclaiming benefits if the claimant stops working.

- Suggested solutions include: simplifying the rules; automatically re-instating old benefits; raising awareness and knowledge of DWA among the wide range of people and organisations who support disabled workers; and targeting information in different formats to particular groups of potential claimants.

3 Findings from the eligibility audit

- Respondents had been working in their current job for an average of just under six years.

- The vast majority of respondents usually worked 16 hours a week or more, and only three per cent worked less than 16 hours a week.

- Nearly all respondents earned less than £150 a week. The median weekly earnings for the sample as a whole was £108 a week net.

- At the time of the fieldwork, just over one-third of respondents were receiving one or more Qualifying Benefits (QBs). Thirty-five per cent were receiving DLA, with only three per cent or fewer receiving any of the other QBs. Only 14 per cent had received QBs immediately before starting their current job.

- Eight per cent of respondents currently received DWA and a further six per cent had received DWA in the past, but were not currently doing so.

- Ten per cent of respondents who gave details of personal savings reported having no savings, while just over one-third reported savings of £3,000 or less. Of the remainder, very few reported having savings in excess of £16,000.

- In addition to the eight per cent of the sample who were already receiving DWA, a further 20 per cent were classified as potentially eligible for DWA. Respondents working in local authority or voluntary agency sheltered workshops were more than twice as likely to be potentially eligible for DWA compared to SEA employees. They were also more than three times as likely to be potentially eligible compared to respondents working in workshops run by Remploy.

- The most important factors affecting eligibility were found to be receipt of QBs and the level of employees earnings. Relaxing the rules on QBs altogether would increase the number of people in the sample who are eligible for DWA by an estimated 40 per cent.

- Over half of all respondents classified as potentially eligible had incomes which took them over the threshold at which they would taper off DWA, although the analysis suggests that income thresholds would have to be raised by at least 20 per cent in order to have any substantial impact on eligibility.

- Other aspects of the qualification criteria did not have a significant effect on eligibility among this group. Relaxing the requirement that people should be working for at least 16 hours a week increased the proportion of those classified as potentially eligible by only two per cent. Relaxing the rules on receipt of QBs during the eight weeks prior to starting their current job (for those who do not receive any current QBs) only increased eligibility by a further one per cent.

- Among the respondents classified as potentially eligible for DWA, almost half were found to be eligible for benefit but not claiming. This means that, among the sample as a whole, eight per cent of workers were classified as eligible non-recipients. (This proportion cannot be accurately grossed up to the wider population of all workers in supported employment because of the way the sample was selected.)

- The incidence of people being eligible for DWA but not claiming was highest among workers in local authority/independent workshops and SEAs.

- The amounts of DWA which we estimate eligible non-recipients would be able to claim range from £1.77 to £61.28 per week. For just under 20 per cent of this group, the amount of benefit would be less than £10 per week; over 10 per cent were entitled to benefit of between £30 and £40 per week; a further seven per cent would be entitled to £50 or more.

4 Findings from group discussions and interviews with employees

- Group and individual interviews were carried out with disabled workers who, based on the eligibility audit, were either eligible to claim DWA and were not doing so, or who had been in receipt of QBs but whose earnings were outside the scope of the benefit.

- Experiences and perceptions of benefits in terms of claiming, understanding eligibility criteria, and the means of obtaining information were considerably varied. Most disabled workers had only a limited knowledge of the range of benefits available for disabled people.

- Less than a third of the respondents recalled ever having heard about DWA. For those who did have some awareness of DWA, this information had mostly been obtained via their employers.

- Perceptions of the purpose of DWA ranged from total non-comprehension to a view that it provided a subsidy for expenses incurred in going to work (e.g. travel expenses), or that it was a benefit aimed at part-time disabled workers and people who are more severely disabled. Hardly any of the respondents recognised DWA as a benefit designed to supplement earnings and encourage people to move into, or remain in, work.

- Access to advice and information about benefits also appeared to be limited for this group. Disabled workers rarely approached official agencies with general questions about their eligibility for benefits although some would make enquiries about a specific benefit, usually to the Benefits Agency. Very few were aware of the availability of the Benefit Enquiry Line (BEL).

- Disabled workers were more inclined to look to people and organisations (e.g. social workers, disability organisations or key workers in sheltered workshops/SEAs) with whom they were already in contact in order to search out information on benefits which they might be able to claim.

- A number of reasons for not claiming DWA were identified including: low awareness of, and lack of understanding about, the benefit; difficulties in locating reliable sources of advice; people's previous experiences of claiming benefits and their lack of confidence in the chances of being able to claim successfully; the complexity of the claims process and, especially, the DWA claim forms and guidance notes; and a general perception that DWA does not apply to people working in supported employment.

- A number of suggestions were made for ways of making it easier for people to claim DWA. These included: improving access to, and publicity about, advice and information services such as Benefits Agency telephone help lines; targeting of information about DWA on relatives, guardians, social workers and key workers in sheltered workshops and SEAs; setting up a body with specific responsibility for advising disabled people about benefits; and automatic notification of potential eligibility for registered disabled people and people receiving QBs.

- Participation in the interviews and group discussions had encouraged a few people to try and find out more about DWA, although they would still need access to advice and practical assistance in order to claim.

I. INTRODUCTION

1.1 Background   DWA was introduced in April 1992. Its aim is to help people start or remain in work by supplementing income from earnings.

DWA may help job-seekers or workers in two ways. First, when disabled people are able to find paid employment either their earnings or their productivity may be lower than average. In this case DWA acts as a wage subsidy for a worker who might otherwise be better off remaining on benefits. Second, DWA may also provide an opportunity to adjust to rejoining the labour force, giving both the disabled person and their employer the chance to try out a job.

DWA is paid for six months irrespective of most changes in circumstances during that time. The benefit is open to GB residents if they are working for 16 hours per week or more in a paid job that is expected to last for more than five weeks. To be eligible people must have been getting one of a range of QBs at any time in the eight weeks before they claim DWA, or be getting one of a different range of QBs at the time they claim. The QB rules are that people should:

EITHER:

- be currently receiving Disability Living Allowance (DLA), Attendance Allowance (AA), Industrial Injuries Disablement Benefit with Constant Attendance Allowance (CAA), a War Disablement Pension with CAA or mobility supplement, or an Invalid Carriage (or other vehicle supplied by DSS)

OR:

- have been in receipt, for at least one day during the eight weeks prior to making their claim, of Incapacity Benefit (IB) (or, formerly, Invalidity Benefit (IVB)), Severe Disablement Allowance (SDA) or a disability premium with Income Support (ISdp), Housing Benefit or Council Tax Benefit.

In addition, claimants have to be aged 16 years or over, have an illness or disability that puts them at a disadvantage in getting a job, be earning less than the DWA income threshold (after household composition and income has been taken in to account), and have £16,000 or less family savings.

A number of changes to DWA were introduced in 1995 which were designed to provide further incentives for people to start or remain in work:

- automatic exemption from National Health Service (NHS) charges for people with savings of £8,000 or less
- an increase in the rate of benefit for couples and lone parents
- an increase in the earnings threshold for single people
- the introduction of a new disabled child's allowance
- the extension of DWA to people undertaking training for work
- an allowance of £10 per week for people working 30 hours or more a week.

As with Family Credit, the amount of DWA which a person receives depends on the total income of the claimant's family. Once the amount to be received has been established, this is normally paid for 26 weeks regardless of most changes in their income or other circumstances.

A unique feature of this benefit is the two-year 'linking rule' which is intended to allow people claiming DWA to return to a long-term incapacity benefit without serving the usual 28-week qualifying period (provided that they still satisfy the criteria for the benefit they were formerly receiving).

Take-up of DWA has been low. When the benefit was first introduced it was anticipated that there would be an average case load of around 50,000. However, the actual take-up of the benefit has never begun to approach this level, and in January 1996 (the last full quarter for which figures are available) there were only 8,340 DWA recipients (DSS, 1996).

The central aims for this study were to examine whether there are eligible non-recipients or potential recipients of DWA in supported employment and, if there are, to investigate ways in which take-up among this group might be increased.

1.2 Structure of the report

This section of the report gives essential background to the study including a discussion of the aims and objectives for the research, and an outline of the research strategy and methods. Section 2 presents the findings from interviews with key workers in the case study sheltered workshops and Supported Employment Agencies (SEAs), and Section 3 provides findings based on the analysis of data from the DWA eligibility audit in the case study sites. Section 4 provides findings from group and individual interviews with employees. Finally, Section 5 summarises the main findings and conclusions from the research.

1.3 Policy issues informing the aims of the study

There are a range of policies aimed at addressing the difficulties which many disabled people face in finding and keeping a job. These include: the provision of rehabilitation and placement services; measures aimed at encouraging good practice among employers; quota schemes; subsidised/sheltered employment; the provision of in-work benefits aimed at reducing the potential financial disincentives to employment arising from the relative levels of benefits and earnings; and, more recently, anti-discrimination legislation (Berthoud, Lakey and McKay, 1993; Dalgleish, 1991; Gooding, 1995; Thornton and Lunt, 1995).

This study focuses on one of these policy measures – in-work benefits – for one particular group of disabled people working in supported employment. Interest in potential take-up of, and eligibility for, DWA among this group was prompted by early findings from a larger programme of research which Policy Studies Institute (PSI) has been undertaking for the DSS as part of their evaluation of DWA (Rowlingson and Berthoud, 1996). In particular, given that the earnings of disabled people in supported employment are generally thought to be relatively low it seemed possible that there may be a potential source of eligible non-claimants among this group. Consequently, the DSS commissioned this smaller self-contained study to investigate this possibility further.

The earlier PSI research (Rowlingson and Berthoud, 1996) identified three main reasons for the low number of people receiving DWA:

i) Ineligibility   Evidence suggests that job retention among disabled people is good. Many disabled employees may well have been in their jobs for a considerable time. If they are not receiving any of the QBs they will not be eligible for DWA. According to the current rules of the benefit, these people could only become eligible for DWA if they first successfully claimed one of the QBs which are paid irrespective of a person being in work (e.g. DLA), or if they left employment, received one of the other QBs, found work again and then claimed DWA within eight weeks.

Some workers may be working less than 16 hours a week and so will not be eligible for DWA. These people could become eligible for DWA if they increased their hours or if the eligibility rules were altered to bring people working under 16 hours in to the scope of the benefit. Some people may be earning too much to come within the scope of the benefit. These people may become eligible if their earnings are reduced or if the earnings thresholds for the benefit were increased.

ii) Non-take-up   Those who are eligible for DWA may not be aware of, or understand, the benefit. Eligible non-recipients may feel that they would be worse off if they claim DWA because of the effects on other benefits such as Housing Benefit or Council Tax Benefit.

iii) Low rate of transition off benefits   In addition to the factors outlined above, the very low rate of transition from long-term incapacity benefits to work was also identified as an important underlying reason for the low numbers of DWA recipients. In the context of the current eligibility rules, this means that only a small number of people are likely to be able to qualify for DWA through receipt of one of the QBs during the eight weeks prior to starting work.

1.4 Aims of the study

The central aim of the study was to examine whether there are eligible non-recipients or potential recipients of DWA in supported employment and, if there are, how these people can be encouraged to claim DWA. To achieve this aim, several questions needed to be answered:

- How many disabled people in supported employment are current recipients of DWA?

- How many are eligible non-recipients of DWA?
  – Why are they not receiving the benefit?
  – What would encourage them to claim the benefit?

- How many are not eligible for the benefit?
  – Why are they not eligible?
  – Are they 'potentially eligible'?
  – What would have to change to make them eligible?

- Who are 'key workers' in supported employment?
  – What role do they play?
  – Can these people be used to increase awareness of DWA among employees and disabled job-seekers?

1.5 Research strategy and methods

The study has been carried out in two main parts which reflect the main aims for the research. First, one part of the study has focused on disabled people in supported employment. In particular, we have focused on questions such as: how many disabled people in supported employment are potentially eligible for DWA; how many claim and/or receive the benefit; and what factors would encourage increased take-up among those who do not claim DWA? The answers to these questions have been sought by means of an eligibility audit survey and follow-up interviews with disabled people in supported employment. Second, the study has also examined the role of key workers (such as factory managers, supervisors, and placement officers) in sheltered workshops/factories and SEAs. Specifically, the research has examined the kinds of practical support and advice about claiming benefits – particularly DWA – which these workers provide to disabled people, and the extent to which they might be able to help with encouraging more people to claim the benefit. Further details of how each part of the study has been carried out are given below.

1.5.1 The role of key workers

In designing the methodology for the study, we anticipated that, although the focus of the study would be on disabled people in supported employment, we would also be heavily reliant on the participation and co-operation of managers and key workers in sheltered workshops and SEAs who were in direct contact with disabled employees. This was necessary, not only to gain access to disabled employees, but also to identify what kind of support such workers might be able to offer in terms of raising awareness about DWA and encouraging take-up of the benefit.

1.5.2 Involving disabled people

From the outset, we recognised that interviews with managers and key workers alone were unlikely to provide sufficient information to answer all the research questions identified for this study. In particular, managers and key workers were unlikely to be able to provide information about employees' households which would be necessary for calculating eligibility for DWA (e.g. details of partners' incomes; household size and composition; and savings). For this reason, we also aimed to carry out a thorough audit of disabled employees' eligibility for DWA, using a self-completion questionnaire. In addition, we wanted to carry out focus group discussions and/or interviews with employees which would enable people to discuss their views on DWA in depth.

1.5.3 Case study selection and screening survey

Before selecting case studies for the research we first needed to gather as much information as possible about the type and extent of variation between sheltered workshops and SEAs that should be covered by the study.

In the case of Remploy workshops, Remploy were able to supply detailed centrally held information about employees in each workshop. This enabled us to identify sites which were representative of all Remploy workshops in terms of employee characteristics (i.e. age, sex and types of impairments), average earnings, type of production, size and geographical location.

This kind of detailed information was not available for local authority, voluntary and independent sheltered workshops and SEAs. Consequently, before making any decisions about selection of the case studies we first carried out a postal screening survey of workshops and SEAs to ascertain details about their employees. This involved distributing a screening questionnaire to sheltered workshops and SEAs in three geographical regions with the highest concentration of disabled people in supported employment. The information collected from the survey included the number of disabled employees for each workshop or SEA, their age ranges, the ratio of male and female employees, types of impairments, length of employment, hours worked, and average earnings.

The survey yielded information about almost 5,000 disabled employees which, together with the information supplied by Remploy, was used to select the case studies for the main part of the research on the basis of:

a representativeness (i.e. how the characteristics of employees, in particular SEAs and workshops, compared with the overall profile of disabled people in supported employment)

b potential eligibility for DWA (i.e. hours worked by employees and level of average earnings).

The information from the survey has also been useful for placing the findings from the eligibility audit (which was based on a much smaller sample) in the context of what is known about the characteristics of supported employment workers in general. Further details of the selection methods and the findings from the screening survey are contained in Appendix 1.

1.5.4 Pilot case studies The main part of the research was intended to be based on a total of nine case study sites – three selected from each of the following three main groups: Remploy workshops; local authority, voluntary or independent sheltered workshops; and supported employment agencies. However, because of the exploratory nature of the study it was decided to pilot the research in one site selected from each of these three main groups initially, before making any final decision on proceeding to the next stage. (Further details of this stage of the research are contained in Appendix 1).

1.6 Location of the study

As noted above, the study was intended to be based on a total of nine case studies. In the event, the research only included a total of eight case study sites comprising three sheltered workshops run by Remploy, two run by a local authority or voluntary body, and three SEAs. The reason for the reduction in the number of case studies was that one of the sites dropped out at a late stage, and this did not leave sufficient time to negotiate access to an alternative site without creating serious delays to the research. In addition, one of the SEAs only participated in the first part of the fieldwork (the interviews with key workers) as they were subsequently unable to spare the staff resources needed to assist with the eligibility audit and follow-up interviews with employees.

Of the eight case study sites which were included, two were located in London and the South-East, three in the North-West, two in the East Midlands and one in the West Country. A full list is given below:

Remploy Sheltered Workshop (A), London (*)

Remploy Sheltered Workshop (B), North-West

Remploy Sheltered Workshop (C), North-West

Voluntary Body Sheltered Workshop (A), East Midlands

Voluntary Body Sheltered Workshop (B), South-East (*)

SEA (A), North-West

SEA (B), East Midlands (*) (**)

SEA (C), West Country

Notes: (*) indicates pilot case study; (**) indicates participation in first stage of fieldwork only.

Summary of Key Points

- DWA was introduced in April 1992. The benefit is intended to help some disabled people move into, or remain in, employment.

- Take-up of DWA has been low. The DSS commissioned this study to find out whether there are eligible non-recipients or potential recipients of DWA in supported employment and, if there are, to investigate how these people can be encouraged to claim DWA.

- Earlier research has suggested three main reasons for the low take-up of DWA: non-eligibility; non-take up by people who are eligible for DWA; and the low rate of transition off long-term incapacity benefits.

- The study has included an eligibility audit among a sample of disabled people working in supported employment. The audit survey has been designed to find out about their earnings, benefits and household circumstances, and to examine how many people might be eligible for DWA.

- The study has also examined the role of 'key workers' in supported employment to find out what kind of role they might have in terms of raising awareness, and encouraging take-up, of DWA.

- The main part of the research is based on eight case studies in Remploy and local authority/independent sector sheltered workshops and SEAs.

2.1 The different types of supported employment

There are three main types of supported employment:

- sheltered workshops run by Remploy
- sheltered workshops run by local authorities or voluntary/independent sector agencies
- SEAs.

Each of these three main types are briefly described below. The key difference is between sheltered workshops (both Remploy and local authority/independent workshops) and SEAs. In the former, employees are employed by, and work in, the workshops. Wages are paid for by a combination of the proceeds from the workshops' production output and government subsidy. SEAs, on the other hand, do not employ disabled people directly but seek to place them in jobs with host employers. (Although Remploy do have a separate arm – the Interwork scheme – which also places workers with host employers.)

There are at least around 25,000 employees in supported employment as a whole. Workers in supported employment have a range of impairments, but most of those in SEAs have learning difficulties.

Remploy   Remploy is a centrally managed commercial organisation operating in about 100 factory sites. In 1992, the organisation had a turnover of about £100 million. Remploy employs about 14,000 workers.

Local authority/voluntary organisation workshops   There are about 120 sheltered workshops run by about 100 local authorities, and 25 voluntary organisations which employ about 7,000 workers in total. The workshops are independent from one another. There is a great deal of variation in the size of each workshop. The smallest workshops employ only a handful of staff and have a turnover of about £50,000. The largest workshops employ over 200 staff and have a turnover of over £6 million.

SEAs   These agencies have developed from the Sheltered Placement Scheme whereby disabled people were placed in open employment but often with a government subsidy to the employer. It is difficult to establish any precise figures for the number of disabled people supported by SEAs as there are now a wide range of agencies providing services which come under the broad definition of supported employment. There are currently 158 agencies in England and Wales on the full membership list of the Association for Supported Employment (AfSE) and these agencies are supporting around 4,000 or 5,000 people. At the same time, the AfSE estimate that only half of the organisations which practice supported employment within the Association's definition of the term (which is integration in a regular work setting) are currently members of AfSE.

2.2 Who are the key workers in supported employment?

As noted above, the design of the research was heavily reliant on the participation and co-operation of managers and key workers in sheltered workshops and SEAs who were in direct contact with disabled employees. The first step, therefore, was to identify who the key workers in the different forms of supported employment were, and what type of role they might have in supporting and advising disabled employees.

Key workers in sheltered workshops were generally believed to be workshop managers, although managers in some of the larger sheltered workshops were likely to have considerably less direct contact with disabled employees. The main role of key workers in sheltered workshops was thought primarily to be to ensure that the organisation continued to produce the goods or services which kept it in business.

Key workers in SEAs, however, were not generally believed to be employers or managers. Their role was thought to be to provide support and help for disabled people who were either referred to the agency or who referred themselves, including, for example, help and support in finding work.

Key workers were believed to be important to the research for two main reasons: first, key workers would be able to provide useful information about employees in their workshop or scheme, including information about hours worked and earnings of their employees; and, second, they might play a major role in providing information and advice to employees, including information and advice about DWA.

The aim of the interview survey of key workers in sheltered workshops and SEAs was to examine the following questions:

- Who are 'key workers' in supported employment?

- What role do they play in supporting and advising disabled employees and/or job-seekers?

- What do they see as the main advantages and disadvantages of DWA for disabled people in supported employment?

- Can these workers be used as a resource for increasing awareness and/or take-up of DWA among disabled employees and job-seekers?

This section of the report contains a discussion of the key findings from the interviews with key workers. Results of the detailed analysis of the interview transcripts are summarised in Appendix 2. These findings suggest that the assumptions which we made about key workers are broadly true, but there is widespread variation in the ways in which they interpret their roles and the extent to which they are prepared to give information and advice about benefits, including DWA. The survey findings also highlight a number of barriers to take-up of DWA. Some of these barriers are seen as resulting from the nature of the benefit itself (e.g. eligibility rules), and some are related to the role of sheltered workshops, SEAs and other agencies who work with this group of disabled people. Finally, this section of the report also examines key workers' views on how some of these barriers might be removed.

2.3 Other agencies key workers are in contact with

Employment referrals to the case study workshops and agencies tend to come from a fairly narrow range of sources (see Table 1 below). This is particularly true of Remploy and local authority/independent sheltered workshops, where referrals are almost exclusively from the Employment Service (ES). Key workers in SEAs, on the other hand, mentioned social services most often. They took referrals from the ES but also reported a number of referrals from other agencies such as the community psychiatric nursing service and Adult Training Centres.

SEAs are also more likely to refer clients on to a wider range of agencies for benefits advice. (This finding is discussed in more detail later in this report.) It would appear, therefore, that key workers in sheltered workshops are comparatively more 'isolated' and, not surprisingly, this may have an important bearing on their ability to access advice and assistance relating to claims for DWA or other benefits.

Table 1   Source of employment referrals

Number of key workers mentioning each source:	Remploy	Workshop	SEAs	All
Social services	0	2	7	9
ES/PACTs/DEAs	4	3	5	12
Health services	0	0	1	1
Training providers	1	0	2	3
Self-referrals	0	1	3	4
Total number of sources	5	6	18	29

2.4 Key workers' role in support and advice-giving about benefits

Not surprisingly, given the organisations' contrasting functions, key workers vary in the degree to which they provide different kinds of support to disabled employees. While the majority of staff interviewed in SEAs had a direct role in supporting employees and job-seekers as part of their usual work activity, workers in sheltered workshops (both Remploy and local authority/independent) worked in management positions which, primarily, involved administration and production rather than any formal employee support role. This is not to say that workshop staff did not take any interest in the welfare of their employees; nor that they never got involved in advising or assisting people to claim benefit. However, it is absolutely clear that there was a marked contrast between workshops and SEAs in the extent to which this is a part of their regular activities.

Workers in the SEAs were also more likely to provide vocational guidance and support with job placements (which, for most, is their main role in any case). Staff in sheltered workshops, on the other hand, were more likely to provide workplace supervision (see Table 2).

The nature of the support given also means that staff in sheltered workshops tended to have more regular contact with employees, whereas the level of contact between employees and SEA staff tended to be more variable.

Table 2   Type of support given to disabled employees by key workers

Numbers of key workers providing each type of support:	Remploy	Workshops	SEAs	All
Vocational guidance	2	1	7	10
Workplace supervision	3	2	4	9
Job placement	1	1	8	10
Benefits advice	1	1	9	12
(Base)	(4)	(3)	(9)	(16)

Table 3   Type of benefits advice and assistance given to disabled employees by key workers

Numbers of key workers providing each type of support:	Remploy	Workshops	SEAs	All
Help with claims forms	1	2	7	10
Advice on individual eligibility/entitlement	1	0	5	6
Advocacy	0	0	2	2
General advice only	2	1	0	3
None	2	1	0	3
(Base)	(4)	(3)	(9)	(16)

At first sight this might suggest that key workers in sheltered workshops are better placed to advise employees about benefits and related financial matters on a one-to-one basis. However, in practice, this is not the case. All of the key workers interviewed had been called upon for help or advice about benefits, including DWA, at times. However, the degree to which they were asked for such help by employees, as well as their ability and willingness to provide it, varied considerably from site to site and between different members of staff in each organisation.

In particular, there is a clear distinction between SEAs and workshops. While all of the key workers in SEAs reported that they do provide advice on benefits, only two out of three workers in independent workshops and one out of four in Remploy workshops did so (see Table 3). There are several reasons for this difference.

First, key workers in sheltered workshops reported an organisational belief that their workplace was *work-based* rather than a *welfare-based* (although the worker at one of the Remploy factories did add that employees do have access to benefits advice from both the personnel office and union representative). This might explain to some extent their hesitation to become involved in benefits issues, although they reported that they were asked by employees for information and advice about benefits from time-to-time, and personally believed that they should try to help when asked:

> '*I think you have to if they feel there's nowhere else they can turn.*'

> '*If they had a difficulty in trying to fill them in [claim forms] we would help, yes. But we don't over-encourage that because we have 75 people here, and we could spend all day filling out forms.*'

Second, practically all of the key workers in sheltered workshops emphasised that they did not have sufficient expertise to give anything more than general advice about benefits. Consequently, unlike key workers in the SEAs, they did not tend to give any detailed advice or assistance on a one-to-one basis and rarely got involved with helping to process claims. Additionally, because it was not generally seen as part of their role, key workers in sheltered workshops were less likely than SEA staff to have any training in benefits advice:

> '*If my knowledge of facilities was better I probably would be able to advise, yes. I do, as I say, have a lot to do with the families who phone me up and say they've got this problem and that problem, and all I can do is offer a sort of counselling service at the moment but there may well be facilities that I could point them towards. A lot of people don't have social workers, have never even thought of contacting social workers or there's a stigma of having a social worker so they bungle through life as best they can, and yes it would be useful to be able to offer real advice but again there's no training within to give me the tools to go out with.*'

> '*We're not experts in benefits, as a matter of fact we have no more knowledge of benefit than most other employers would have.*'

Third, key workers in sheltered workshops did not tend to gather personal information formally about employees, and mostly reported that they would be reluctant to actively seek such information. However, they generally seemed to know a certain amount of detail about their employees, mainly because most of them work in the same workshop for a long time. For example, some of the workers said that they would mostly know whether or not an employee was married and had children, but were less likely to know about their household income or what benefits they received (although the key worker at one of the Remploy factories reported that some of this information was held at the site office but was not passed on to factory staff). In fact, only one out of the seven sheltered workshop staff interviewed said that they would usually know details of employees' benefits but, even so, did not always have full details of their household circumstances. In the words of two of the key workers:

'I don't delve into any details – specific details – of what they're claiming. As an employer, to a certain extent it's not my business to enquire about those things. We do know quite a lot about some individuals and what they're claiming but, as I say, the problem is we have a dual role – not only do we have the social side, but the most important thing is we are an employer, so as such we've got to be very careful that we don't appear to pry.'

'I don't know specific details of benefits, because, let's be honest, they are employees, and they have their right to their own secrecy – we're not part of the social services, in effect. But as an employer, for me to ask personal details is an intrusion on what they're doing, but I do know quite a lot about what they're actually receiving. A proportion receive Mobility Allowance, probably of the 75 here, only eight or nine, maybe anything up to 10 or 11 may receive Mobility. A large proportion receive Housing Benefit and other supplementary benefits associated with that. One or two get free transport...so they receive a range of benefits, I think.'

Staff in the SEAs, on the other hand, are obliged to ensure that people do not experience any financial disadvantage if they are found suitable employment. As a result, key workers usually attempted to gather relevant details about benefits and household finances from all clients. This meant that, compared to staff in sheltered workshops, they were better placed to offer advice about benefits:

'I do vocational profiling, so we're looking at someone holistically, doing their benefits and suchlike, their own experiences, and marrying that up to a job. My brief is that people have to be better off by working, not just a good feel factor, so I wouldn't put them at financial risk and suchlike. I then market for those people, then match outcomes with what people are looking for.'

'If I think they're entitled to something then I will point them in the right direction, and if they need a bit of extra help I would tap in to what's around. ...for example, if it's a part-time job over 16 hours, and it's likely to last more than five weeks, then I would advise DWA unless they are...they're earning too much so it's over the £104.80, let's say, for take home pay.'

However, as with staff in sheltered workshops, key workers in the SEAs differed both in their level of knowledge about benefit entitlement, and in the extent to which they were prepared to give detailed advice on an individual basis. Where SEA staff were relatively less involved with benefits advice this was most likely to be because of lack of confidence in the level of their knowledge or, in particular, concern about the possibility of giving clients the wrong advice. Some also reported that there are conflicting pressures caused by the need to place clients in employment as quickly as possible. This sometimes means that there is insufficient time to give full consideration to a client's financial position at the time they have their initial assessment, and some clients might miss the opportunity to claim DWA as a result.

With the exception of the supervisor at one of the Remploy factories, all of the key workers interviewed were, at a minimum, prepared to give information about DWA. For example, they might tell people that there was a benefit called DWA. Most were also prepared to offer some level of practical help from time-to-time. For example, some would help people to fill in claim forms, while others would go to the benefits agency with claimants. However, as with benefits advice in general, there are some noticeable differences between staff in the SEAs and workshops.

For example, more than half of the key workers in SEAs reported that the support they give to clients includes one-to-one advice on eligibility and entitlement to DWA, compared to only one of the workers in the workshops. Where SEA staff do not give individual advice on eligibility and entitlement this is usually either because of pressure of work, or because they lack sufficient knowledge. However, it is worth noting that some also pointed out that the issue does not arise that often because – in their view at least – so few of their clients are likely to be eligible for DWA in any case. It is also important to note that, while staff in the SEAs are much more likely to be involved with benefits advice, they do not, on the whole, see themselves as experts in this area. Rather, while it is often part of their role to consider a client's financial situation, their main activity is primarily focused on placing them in employment. Moreover, as noted earlier, this primary role may even run counter to their potential role in encouraging take-up of DWA as their aim is to secure employment for clients at the maximum wages possible. In fact, one or two actually pointed out that, in one sense, they hoped that their clients would fail to qualify for DWA as this would mean they had been successful in meeting their primary objectives. In the words of one key worker:

> '[Giving benefits advice] isn't particularly our role, and I work quite closely with two social work teams, and they're very clued up on benefits which I suppose makes me a bit lazy, and they quite often will take over the role of applying for benefits which I'm happy to let them do. I've been fortunate this last year. I've placed quite a few people in quite high paid jobs where they just lose the benefits, and there's no issues around DWA or something like that. It's high income; it's clear cut. I prefer it to be like that because it's better for everyone.'

Similarly, among key workers in sheltered workshops the main reasons given for not advising on entitlement and eligibility for DWA were: (a) they did not see this as their role; (b) concern about giving incorrect information or advice; and, (c), lack of knowledge about DWA.

These findings from the interviews clearly indicate that key workers in supported employment organisations can be seen as a potential resource for raising awareness about, and/or encouraging take-up of, DWA. It is equally clear, however, that there would need to be greater incentives and support to enable them to realise this potential.

Key workers in all of the case study sites reported that they do refer queries about DWA and other benefits to agencies who are believed to be qualified to give expert advice and information. The main sources of referral for general benefits information are the Benefits Agency, ES and Citizens Advice Bureaux (see Table 4). The Benefits Agency and Citizens Advice Bureaux were also the most frequently source of referrals for information on DWA. A little surprisingly, perhaps, key workers are much less likely to refer to the ES if they have queries about DWA. This is partly because they have fewer potential claimants for DWA compared to other benefits. At the same time, some of the key workers did specifically mention that they had not found ES staff to be particularly knowledgeable and/or helpful when they had used them in the past.

Table 4   Sources of external benefits advice used by key workers

Numbers of key workers referring employees to each source:	For general benefits information	For information on DWA
Benefits Agency	11	8
CABx	9	6
ES/PACTs/DEAs	10	2
Local advice centres	3	2
Social Services	4	2
Disability organisations	3	0
Others	1	2
(Base)	(16)	(16)

In contrast to this, several workers – particularly in SEAs – reported that they often refer to the local Benefits Agency if they have queries they cannot handle alone. Workers in SEAs found this assistance valuable. Key workers also particularly welcomed having a named contact, either at the Benefits Agency or a local advice centre, whom they could telephone with any questions or problems. In most cases, this was primarily related to the practical need for information – often on individual cases. However, there is also an important subjective dimension to this kind of support, as building a good working relationship with these contacts helps to give key workers greater confidence when dealing with enquiries about DWA or other benefits:

Staff at one of the SEAs also attended a monthly 'benefits surgery' organised by the local Benefits Agency. This was felt to be very helpful, both for the staff themselves and – indirectly – for their clients.

It was also noticeable that key workers in the SEAs tended to refer to a wider range of outside agencies compared to staff in the sheltered workshops. As noted earlier, staff in sheltered workshops also tended to take employment referrals from a narrower range of agencies and, in this sense, they were comparatively more 'isolated' than staff in the SEAs. This may also have had an impact on their ability to advise employees on DWA and other benefits as they had fewer sources to turn to. This relative isolation also appears to be reflected in the way in which they used these outside agencies in relation to benefits advice. For example, while they might have been in contact with DEAs and PACTs, it appears that this contact was often restricted to employment related matters as staff were far less likely to mention them as a source of advice on DWA.

A few of the key workers had used the DWA helpline and mostly found this useful for clarifying issues on entitlement for particular employees or clients. One of the SEA workers, however, reported receiving 'inconsistent' advice when using this service. Again, it is also noticeable that staff in the SEAs are more likely to know about and use the helpline than those in sheltered workshops. Although they varied in the extent to which they were willing to become directly involved in advice giving, all of the key workers recognised that their employees or clients have a need for help with claiming benefits. This was not only because of their household circumstances (i.e. the majority of people in supported employment were single with no children and lived on their own), but also because many had low levels of literacy. Consequently, according to the key workers, many would face difficulties with dealing with claims forms for DWA and other benefits. Nevertheless, most people were thought to have someone who could help them to claim benefits, for example, a social worker, carer, relative or friend.

2.5 Key workers' knowledge of DWA

Most of the key workers had received the DWA information and claim packs and other leaflets about DWA from the Benefits Agency. The only two workers who had not received this information were in Remploy factories, although one of the Remploy sites had received the information via their group headquarters.

Views on the value of the information on DWA were quite mixed. Two of the key workers thought that the information was both very useful and easy to understand and prepared them adequately for discussing DWA with their clients. On the other hand, two other key workers thought more or less the precise opposite. The majority reported that the information had been useful, but with some qualification. In most cases, this was because, although they could see the need for some kind of documentation, it was felt that it would be of more help to them if it was simpler and easier to understand. Some (particularly staff in the sheltered workshops) also thought that the documentation was of limited use in practice as they had so few enquiries about DWA in any case. One or two workers also commented that they preferred to have direct and personal contact with staff at the Benefits Agency if they had any queries on DWA as this was a much more effective way of getting the information they needed.

Less than half of the key workers had attended any training or briefing sessions on DWA. Again, views on the value of this training were quite mixed. Two of the workers thought that the training they had received was very useful as an introduction to DWA, but two did not find it useful at all, and one found the content difficult to understand.

As noted earlier, although key workers were prepared to advise on DWA, several were not particularly confident about their knowledge of the benefit. However, it is also interesting to note that some of those who said they were unsure about their ability to give advice on DWA did in fact advise employees on other benefits such as Mobility Allowance. Given that DWA is still relatively new, this suggests that at least some key workers might become more confident about advising on DWA as they become more used to the benefit. Another reason for suggesting this possibility is that, while they may have expressed a lack of confidence, the responses to specific questions about different aspects of DWA indicate that some of the workers probably have a better understanding of the benefit than they realise. For example, some had an accurate idea about the QBs for DWA, while others also knew about the eight-week qualifying period and/or the two-year linking rule. Key workers' overall grasp of the purpose of the benefit and who was likely to be eligible to claim was also reasonably accurate in the light of the findings from the eligibility audit. For example, most believed that many disabled people in supported employment would not be eligible for DWA, either because they earned too much, or because they failed to meet the requirement that they should be in receipt of a QB.

2.6 Perceived advantages of DWA

Key workers reported two main advantages of DWA. First, the benefit is seen as a useful top-up or boost for the income of disabled people on low wages. However, this is seen as only applying to a small number of disabled people in supported employment on very low wages, and key workers' (albeit limited) experience of helping people to claim the benefit led them to believe that most would not qualify. At the same time, only a few stated that they wanted to see the earnings threshold for the benefit raised to enable more people to qualify. Some were actually opposed to this idea because they thought that it might create a disincentive for people to try to increase their earnings.

Second, some key workers also welcomed the protection offered to disabled people by the two-year linking rule as employees' concerns about the perceived threat to their existing benefits was often mentioned (by key workers) as one of the obstacles to take-up of DWA. Some also wanted to see this protection extended to all disabled people returning to work – providing a safety net even after an employee has gone past the earnings threshold. They did not, however, wish to see the two-year time-period for which protection was offered extended; this was mainly because they felt that after two years people were very likely to continue working and would no longer require the protection.

More generally, DWA was perceived as providing an incentive to enter employment by a few of the key workers, although one or two also pointed out that the benefit's potential as a bridge between benefit and work has not yet been realised.

Lastly, three out of the 16 key workers interviewed said that they did not think DWA offered any advantages at all for people in supported employment. This was because they felt that the benefit was simply too complicated – particularly for people with learning difficulties.

2.7 Perceived disadvantages of DWA and barriers to increasing take-up

Key workers perceived a number of disadvantages associated with DWA. Those which were mentioned most frequently were related to: the perceived complexity of the benefit and the application process; a lack of awareness and understanding about the purpose of DWA as an in-work benefit; and the level at which current DWA earnings thresholds are set. These are discussed in more detail below.

2.7.1 Understanding DWA

DWA was thought to be complicated both for key workers and for claimants to understand – particularly the eligibility criteria and especially the qualifying benefits. Key workers suggested that the eligibility criteria should be simplified by, for example, reducing or scrapping the rules relating to QBs.

Further, several key workers emphasised that employees often have difficulty understanding the concept of an in-work benefit like DWA and, consequently, tend to assume that it does not apply to them.

2.7.2 Completing the claim forms

The various claim forms were thought to be too long and too complicated, particularly because of the large proportion of people in supported employment who have learning difficulties or who have low levels of literacy. In the words of two key workers:

'My main problem on the DWA form is where it asks what other benefits are being received, and most of them can't remember what benefits they get. Somebody along the way, a social worker or somebody, has filled in a form for them, and they get a benefit, and it goes into the bank, and they don't know how it started and they don't know how much it is.'

'The reason it doesn't work is the complexity of the forms. The forms in themselves are not complex, but the sheer number of pages are. There's a lot of pages, a lot of information required and, in order to be eligible to fill the form in, you already have to have filled in a whole host of other forms on the basis that you need to have had some other benefit.'

In addition, some key workers were concerned that the Employer's DWA form (EEF200) might discourage potential employers from employing disabled people. This was mainly because the form was long and had to be completed every six months. Key workers also thought the requirement that claimants had to submit a new claim form every six months was bureaucratic and potentially off-putting for claimants and employers. In contrast, however, some key workers thought that employers should be giving more information about DWA and encouraging more people to claim.

One key worker stated that the provision of the same ready-reckoners which are used by Benefits Agency staff when calculating benefits would be of use when they were advising clients. In fact, one key worker had already obtained a ready-reckoner.

2.7.3 Claiming and reclaiming

Reclaiming benefits if people were unable to continue working or decided that they did not want to continue working was also thought to be problematic. Some key workers in SEAs also thought that this was a particular disincentive for people moving in and out of employment. Some suggested that benefits should be issued automatically if a person stopped working within two years rather than requiring people to reclaim their previous benefits – if they still existed. In the words of two key workers:

'The wording on it [the DSS claim pack] is such as you may be able to reclaim your benefits if, within two years, if you gave up work for some reason. So people think, "I don't want to lose my benefit; I don't want to run that risk." What I'd like to see is, on reclaims, not having to go through the whole pro forma again – just to say, "No change", or, "Yes, there have been changes; these are the changes" – because it's a very comprehensive form. And reclaiming benefits, I just don't understand why it has to be so complicated. What I'd like to see is, if somebody had to reclaim benefit who was getting DWA, and it is within the two years, so they just submit the sick note to be accepted, and then the reclaim would just go ahead automatically, instead of having to jump through all the hoops again.'

'This is another one of these you have to go through every six months. That's another one of the problems: it's one of these situations where you see a fear that people on disability – with disabilities – have who are on benefits is that they're going to lose the benefits they've already got because people have done of recent times. They've been on a benefit, they get a job, holding it down for a few months, lose it, and then they don't go back on to the benefits they were previously on because the regime that sets the benefit up in the first place has been changed. So it's a huge disincentive to people to go to work because of the risk if they lose their job so it is with this benefit. If they're £5 a week better off for working and getting this benefit, the risk they impose upon themselves is very significant. So if they get £5 a week more for working as opposed to not working and have great risks if they lose a job, not getting back on to the level of benefit they're on prior to working, the intelligent ones don't take the risk.'

2.7.4 The 'disabled' label

Key workers in sheltered workshops were concerned that DWA carried a disabled label which might deter people from claiming. They felt that some disabled people were reluctant to describe themselves as disabled, particularly after having achieved the new status which having a job gave them. As a consequence some of them reported difficulties in encouraging people to register as disabled. In the words of one key worker:

'A lot of them don't like claiming anything; they don't like admitting they have a disability. It's terrible to try to get people to register for a green card; nobody knows they've got it. Applying for it admits the fact that they've got a disability, and a lot of them will say – "I'm not disabled, I just can't" – whatever it is.'

Some of the key workers also pointed to difficulties associated with trying to overcome the perceived stigma of receiving benefit. This was felt to be particularly problematic for people in supported employment for whom the aim of working is often as much about 'coming off benefits' as it is about earning a wage. Added to the 'bad press' which some felt the benefit had received in the early stages this may present a significant obstacle to encouraging more people to claim DWA. In the words of one key worker:

'There was a lot of negative publicity around it at the beginning, and we tended not to get deeply involved in it, 'til we saw how the thing was shaking out, and it's only during the last 12 months people have started saying, "Hang on a minute, this might work."'

2.7.5 Earnings thresholds and the perceived 'benefit trap'

Most of the key workers felt that the current earnings thresholds for DWA represent one of the most significant barriers to claiming. Several of the workers also thought that many disabled people seeking employment encountered a *benefits trap* as they were able to get similar amounts in benefits as they would if they worked in supported employment. Some people would decide not to work, and others worked for a short time and then gave up because they found that there was insufficient financial advantage for them to continue working. For example, one key worker reported that only one in three people recruited to jobs in supported employment would stay. The rest would generally leave after a period of about four weeks to six months.

DWA was not thought to offer sufficient financial incentive to encourage some disabled people to seek employment, and very few people in supported employment were thought to be eligible for the benefit in any case (mostly because of their earnings, but also because they did not have qualifying benefits). Some key workers also felt that the first few weeks at work were important in determining whether or not a person would continue working. Others were concerned that any delay between starting work and claiming DWA might act as an additional disincentive to continue working, particularly if a person was unsure whether or not they wanted to work. In the words of a key worker:

> '*I'm in favour of any allowance that enables people with disabilities to get a reasonable living. So I think the only sad part from my meagre knowledge of DWA is that they already have to be qualifying in some way for a benefit to get a top-up benefit. It would suggest that either the first benefit isn't adequate or that it's still missing people who need support. [Employee name] who desperately needs financial support of some sort seems to fall between everything. He's in his 50s, he's a slow learner, and he lives on the breadline. He doesn't qualify for any of the schemes that are around. ...I would have thought that Disability Working Allowance would have been also aimed towards those sorts of people. He is working, he's doing his best, he just cannot get enough, and the fact he doesn't qualify for some other benefit stops him qualifying for this one.*'

The strength of a disabled person's desire to work was thought to be the most important factor in their decision to seek employment and to continue working. Key workers also thought there was a need to consider the influence of others on disabled peoples' expectations about work and their own abilities, including the influence of schools, social workers, and parents and carers.

Key workers in the SEAs reported that many disabled people had realistic and clear ideas about the type of job they wanted and the type of job they could get. Key workers in the sheltered workshops thought that, while some disabled people entered employment with high expectations about the future, they would probably only ever work in supported employment. Some of the workers also expressed concerns about employees who could work in higher paid jobs (either as key workers within the workshop or outside of supported employment altogether) but were discouraged by family and friends from pursuing such career progression in case they lost their benefits. In this sense, the benefits system in general – and DWA in particular – is seen as creating disincentives to work, or to seeking promotion or higher paid employment. Greater links with training and career development were suggested as ways of motivating disabled people in supported employment to seek better paid jobs. Other suggestions included allowing claims for DWA to be made *before* starting work so that claimants can be sure of their overall benefit position before committing themselves.

Several of the key workers felt that there was a need to raise awareness about DWA among disabled people in supported employment. However, although they could see some value in targeting information at disabled people in supported employment, they did not generally think that this could be achieved through simply producing clearer documentation as a large proportion of employees and clients have low literacy levels. In fact, clients were frequently uncertain as to what benefits they were actually receiving. In the words of two key workers:

> '*The applicant I had recently, he wouldn't − there's no way he could − have gone through those forms at all. Because the level of his disability, his reading's very limited, and his understanding, even if I were to read through it and explain it, there's only so much that would have actually been retained. So I had to do it with his mum and with him and myself.*'

> '*I suppose the initial difficulty is that people don't fully understand what benefits they're on. You might ask somebody what benefit they're on, and they might say Income Support but that might actually mean they have SDA. They might get some Income Support, or they might have Housing Benefit as well, or they might have the Community Charge − they might not be paying that. So, people not actually understanding or, if it's something like Disability Living Allowance, not knowing what it's made up of and things like that − so I think that's initially where the difficulties are.*'

Instead key workers recommended a combination of raising awareness among the people who provide support and advice for disabled people in supported employment, and targeting information in different formats to particular groups of potential claimants (e.g. people receiving DLA). In particular, key workers recommended that information should be targeted at two main groups of people: professionals who provide support and advice for disabled people, particularly agencies that provided domiciliary support for disabled people living alone; and families/carers. There were several reasons for suggesting the targeting of information at these groups.

First, key workers were concerned that there might be a lack of awareness about DWA among professionals who provided support and advice for disabled people − including sheltered workshops and SEAs. As noted earlier, some felt that DWA had attracted a bad press in its first year; this was also believed to have generated negative attitudes towards the benefit among professionals which key workers thought needed to be challenged. On the other hand, another view was that by giving key workers a tool such as DWA, they were in effect being encouraged to set their sights lower when seeking employment for clients. In other words, instead of seeking the best possible job for a client, key workers would be encouraged to seek a lower paid job and try to use DWA as a top-up. In the words of one worker:

'I think if you can get their [placement officer's] confidence in using it then I think there's a danger in it. If we get people very confident in using DWA, and very confident in having this tool available, that it may make some folks aim a lot lower or amend their sights about what they're trying to do. We don't want, looking at it in fairly abstract terms, you don't want people settling or going to get folks jobs with DWA when they could have got a better job.'

Second, some key workers felt that parental attitudes towards benefits were often entrenched, and that their involvement in discussions about benefits might affect whether or not a disabled person claimed DWA. They felt that there was a need to raise awareness among parents and carers and to encourage them to investigate the possible benefits of claiming DWA. In the words of one key worker:

'They've been on benefits all their life, and I don't think this comes from individuals. I think this is coming from the parents because the parents have had to fight tooth and nail to get the benefits that they're on. You talk about work and it's, "Oh no, my little Johnnie will never be able to do that, never get the going rate, they'll never be accepted and they'll lose all their benefits, and we're not prepared to sort of fight tooth and nail again because it's taken us all these years to sort them out." It's fear – fear of the unknown – and no matter how many times you say, "That's my job, I'll sort that out" – no, not interested. So obviously the individuals, some of them live at home with the parents, and albeit the individual wants to work, the bottom line is they've got to go home and live with mum and dad, and it's mum and dad really that you need to get on your side to say, "Yeah," win their trust over basically to say, "Look, I can deal with that and I can sort the benefits out for you."'

Third, some of the key workers also suggested that the provision of information about DWA would be improved by better co-ordination between the agencies involved with people in supported employment – particularly DEAs and PACTs. This was seen as having two main advantages: first, people could be advised about DWA before making any decisions about entering employment; and, second, more frequent discussions about the benefit between the different agencies would help to increase understanding and knowledge about DWA.

Fourth, some key workers offered practical suggestions on the ways in which information could be more effectively targeted at disabled people in supported employment. As noted above, simply producing clearer documentation was not seen as the answer (although this would still be welcome). Rather, key workers felt that information would be more effectively disseminated through the television and radio and through the popular (i.e. tabloid) press as these are the sources which disabled people and their carers would more often use. Some also suggested that there might be some value in producing information on DWA in different versions and in different formats aimed at particular groups. This included, for example, more information in accessible formats for people with visual impairments and people with learning difficulties, or specific information for people in receipt of QBs such as DLA. In the words of one key worker:

> 'The local press actually about a month or so ago...there were just little box ads in the recruitment pages, in the jobs section, which I thought again was a good place to put it. But, in saying that, a lot of the applicants we're working with won't...can't, or whatever, look through the papers so they wouldn't necessarily see that. Yes, I think that's great for other people, for some people, because that's where they're going to be looking, but a lot of our applicants can't read, or write or anything, so I don't know. I wonder how much actually goes out to the carers and the support agencies who can then create the awareness with the applicants.'

More generally, several of the key workers felt that there should be a more proactive approach, both to informing people about DWA, and to encouraging take-up. For example, some felt that there should be a greater emphasis on training and practical demonstration sessions for key workers in supported employment (and other professional agencies) as this would be more useful than written information. For disabled employees, suggestions included: having specialist DWA advisors in local Jobcentres or Benefits Agency offices; using outreach benefit officers to raise awareness about DWA in Further Education colleges; and targeting information in places where potential claimants were likely to be found (e.g. special schools, Adult Training Centres). In the words of one key worker:

> 'I think you can't beat face-to-face meetings with people about DWA. I mean even the benefits chap that we speak to . . . I mean we give him a case, and it's, "Apply for DWA, that's the best route." But no-one's actually sat down and explained why it came about, the criteria that you need to meet to qualify for it and the length of time it's given for and why the government introduced it in the first place. But, yeah, I feel that that would be useful rather than handouts or whatever. I mean it sounds as though you're making excuses, but there's so many other things to be getting on with. No one person here is an expert on benefits and it's always been a case of, "Yeah, let's deal with it when it happens – the manual's there and the support is in place." Should we need to find out about it we can do, and I think because it comes out on print, and it's all too easy to say, "I'll read that later on," and you never get round to doing it.'

Summary of Key Points
- There are three main types of supported employment: sheltered workshops run by Remploy; sheltered workshops run by local authorities or voluntary/independent sector agencies; and SEAs.

- The key difference is between sheltered workshops (both Remploy and local authority/independent workshops) and SEAs. In the former, employees are employed by, and work in, the workshops. SEAs, on the other hand, do not employ disabled people directly but seek to place them in jobs with host employers.

- There are about 23,000 employees in supported employment as a whole. Workers in supported employment have a range of impairments, but most of those in SEAs have learning difficulties.

- There is quite a wide variation in the roles that key workers perform in giving advice about benefits. In general, workers in SEAs are more prepared to give advice than those in sheltered workshops.

- Workers in SEAs tended to have more contacts with outside agencies than those in local authority/independent, and especially Remploy, workshops.

- Three main obstacles to key workers advising people about DWA were identified: the fact that some key workers, especially in sheltered workshops, do not see this as part of their role; their concerns about the possibility of giving people incorrect advice; and their lack of detailed knowledge about DWA.

- The main disadvantages to DWA were perceived as: complex rules and claim forms; the 'benefits trap'; the lack of understanding and information about DWA; and the anxiety around, and difficulty of, reclaiming benefits if the claimant stops working.

- Suggested solutions include: simplifying the rules; automatically reinstating old benefits; raising awareness and knowledge of DWA among the wide range of people and organisations who support disabled workers; and targeting information in different formats to particular groups of potential claimants.

3.1 Response rates and respondent characteristics

A total of 270 out of a possible 635 audit questionnaires were completed for this part of the research. This represents an overall response rate of 43 per cent, although the response among particular agencies and workshops varied from 18 per cent to 75 per cent.

A full breakdown of the response rates is given in Table 5. Of the 270 respondents who returned the questionnaire, 70 per cent were male and 30 per cent female.

There was a fairly broad age range among respondents in the sample – from 17 to 69 years of age. The median age across all of the case study sites was 35 years, with SEA employees being the youngest on average and Remploy workshop employees the oldest (See Tables 6 and 7).

The overall age profile of the sample was very similar to that found in the screening survey of all workshops and agencies except that the audit sample had slightly fewer people in the 16 to 29 age group and slightly more people in the 50 plus age group (see Table A1.5 in Appendix 1). There was also a slightly higher proportion of male respondents in the sample compared to the screening survey (70 per cent and 66 per cent respectively). Both surveys also indicated that sheltered workshops have a noticeably higher ratio of male to female employees compared to SEAs.

Table 5   Audit survey: Response rates

Name	Q'aires sent	Q'aires received	Response rate
Trentham (Remploy)	67	12	18
Holloway (Remploy)	67	24	36
Bolton (Remploy)	61	22	36
Peterborough (Workshop)	60	45	75
Leatherhead (Workshop)	48	36	75
Trowbridge (SEA)	300	111	37
Nantwich (SEA)	32	20	63
Totals	635	270	43

Table 6 Age of respondents

Age	Remploy (%)	Workshops (%)	SEAs (%)	All (%)
Under 20	3	0	I	2
20–29	II	21	49	31
30–39	28	25	31	29
40–49	28	31	12	21
50 and over	30	23	7	17
(Base)	(57)	(80)	(125)	(262)
Median (years)	44	42	30	35

Missing cases = 8

Table 7 Respondents' sex

Gender	Remploy (%)	Workshops (%)	SEAs (%)	All (%)
Male	38	82	64	70
Female	20	18	36	30
(Base)	(58)	(80)	(126)	(264)

Missing cases = 6

3.2 Details of respondents' current employment

We asked respondents to record the length of time they had been working in their current job. Of the 270 respondents:

- one per cent had started work in the last eight weeks

- 17 per cent had been working in their current job for between three months and less than two years

- the majority – 69 per cent – had been working in their current job for two years or more

- 13 per cent did not answer.

Respondents had been working in their current job for an average of 5.8 years. There was a significant difference between SEA and workshop employees. The former group had been in their current jobs for an average of under four years, compared to 10 years for the latter group (see Table 8).

The audit sample also tended to have been in their current jobs for longer than respondents to the screening survey (see Table A1.6 in Appendix 1). Ten per cent of the audit sample had been in their current job for up to one year, compared to 22 per cent in the screening survey. Most of this difference can be accounted for by employees from SEAs, only 12 per cent of whom had been in their current job for up to a year, compared to 27 per cent in the screening survey. This might suggest a non-response bias among SEA employees working for a shorter time period as the figures for people working for over a year were very similar for both samples. (The figures for Remploy and local authority/voluntary agency workshops were also fairly similar in both surveys).

Table 8   Length of time in current job

Length of time	Remploy	Workshops	SEAs	All
	(%)	(%)	(%)	(%)
8 weeks or less	2	I	0	I
3 months to I year	7	4	12	9
I year to less than 2 years	5	2	15	8
2 years to less than 5 years	9	I I	27	15
5 years or more	58	81	28	54
Did not answer	19	I	18	13
(Base)	(58)	(81)	(131)	(270)
Median (years)	*10.1*	*10.1*	*3.8*	*5.8*

As expected, the vast majority of respondents usually worked 16 hours a week or more, and only three per cent worked less than 16 hours a week (see Table 9).

Among the sample as a whole 75 per cent usually worked 35 hours or more each week. SEA employees worked the fewest hours, with just over half working 35 hours or more compared to 94 per cent and 100 per cent respectively of employees in local authority/voluntary agency and Remploy workshops.

The highest number of hours usually worked each week was 60 hours and the lowest was five hours. The median number of hours usually worked a week was 38.

Table 9 Average hours worked per week

Age	Remploy	Workshops	SEAs	All
	(%)	(%)	(%)	(%)
Under 16	0	I	5	3
16 to 35	0	5	42	22
Over 35	100	94	53	75
(Base)	(56)	(79)	(127)	(262)
Median (hours)	*38.0*	*39.0*	*37.0*	*38.0*

Missing cases = 8

Similarly, as shown in Table 10, nearly all respondents earned less than £150 a week. The highest amount recorded was £181 and the lowest was only £5. The median amount usually earned by respondents across the case study sites was £108 a week net.

The average earnings among the audit survey sample were lower than the average among all workers in the main DWA evaluation (£113). At the same time their earnings were also higher than the average for all DWA recipients in the main evaluation (£82). However, as the sample in the main DWA evaluation included a larger proportion of people working less than 30 hours, a direct comparison of earnings between the two samples could be slightly misleading. Restricting the comparison to earnings among the audit survey sample and all those working 30 plus hours a week in the main DWA evaluation shows that the former were earning notice-ably less – £108 compared to £149 (Rowlingson and Berthoud, 1996)

The audit sample contained a noticeably smaller proportion of people working less than 16 hours a week compared to the screening survey (three per cent compared with 11 per cent). This is a consequence of the selection process for the survey as the case study sites were specifically selected in order to maximise the possibility of identifying people who are potentially eligible for DWA (that is, by screening out those with a large number of employees working less than 16 hours). The proportion working for 35 hours or more, however, was similar in both surveys (see Table A1.7 in Appendix 1).

Similarly, the audit sample had a higher proportion of people earning less than £100 per week – 40 per cent compared to 30 per cent in the screen-ing survey. There was also a markedly smaller proportion of people earning over £150 per week – three per cent compared to 20 per cent in the screening survey (see Table A1.8 in the Appendix). Again, this is a function of the selection process for the case studies. We deliberately targeted those with a higher proportion of people on low wages on the assumption that they would be more likely to be potentially eligible for DWA.

Table 10 Average weekly take home pay

Earnings (per week)	Remploy (%)	Workshops (%)	SEAs (%)	All (%)
Less than £50	2	4	9	6
£50 to less than £100	2	38	45	34
£100 to less than £150	94	53	43	57
Over £150	2	5	3	3
(Base)	(58)	(81)	(131)	(266)
Median	£118	£108	£95	£108

Missing cases = 4

3.3 Current receipt of QBs

Although we obtained information concerning respondents' current employment from the screening exercise, we had no information about their benefits or household incomes. The audit survey was, therefore, essential for collecting the relevant details necessary for estimating potential eligibility for DWA.

At the time of the fieldwork, just over one-third of respondents were receiving one or more of the QBs. In most cases, the QB which they were receiving was DLA (35 per cent), with only three per cent or fewer receiving any of the other QBs (see Table 11).

Table 11 Receipt of current QBs

Benefit received	Remploy	Workshops	SEAs	All
	(%)	(%)	(%)	(%)
DLA	16	51	33	35
Attendance Allowance	3	4	1	2
War Disablement Pension	2	0	0	1
Industrial Injuries Pension	2	5	1	2
Invalid Three Wheeler	0	0	0	0
(Base)	(58)	(81)	(131)	(270)

Employees in local authority/voluntary agency sheltered workshops were considerably more likely to be in receipt of QBs than the other groups in the sample. For example, 51 per cent of this group received DLA, compared to 33 per cent of SEA employees and only 16 per cent of Remploy employees.

3.4 Current receipt of DWA

Eighteen respondents (eight per cent) said that they currently received DWA. In addition, 14 (six per cent) said that they had received DWA in the past, but were not currently receiving it (see Table 12).

SEA employees were the most likely to be receiving DWA currently (11 per cent compared to eight per cent among the sample as a whole). This is probably associated with the earlier findings on the lower average wages among this group. Both SEA and local authority/voluntary workshop employees were also more likely than Remploy employees to have received DWA in the past. Again, this is consistent with what we would expect from the relative earnings levels among the different groups in the sample.

Table 12 Current and past receipt of DWA

Sheltered employment	Proportions receiving DWA:		
	Current	Past	
	(%)	(%)	(Base)
Remploy	0	2	(49)
Workshops	4	10	(73)
SEAs	11	6	(102)
All	8	6	(224)

Missing = 46

3.5 Receipt of QBs immediately before starting current job

Thirty-eight (14 per cent) of respondents had received one or more QBs during the eight weeks prior to starting their current job:[1]

- nine per cent had received IVB;

- four per cent had received SDA;

- two per cent had received ISdp – although, the fact that 21 per cent received Income Support and that there were several missing values for this item suggests the likelihood that others were also receiving the premium

- three per cent had received Council Tax Benefit with a disability premium or higher pensioner premium (eight per cent received Council Tax Benefit but did not report receiving the premium)

- one per cent had received Housing Benefit with disability premium or higher pensioner premium (seven per cent received Housing Benefit but did not report receiving the premium).

Over half (56 per cent) of the respondents said that they had not received any of these benefits immediately before starting their present job, and five per cent did not know (see Table 13).

SEA and local authority/voluntary sector workshop employees were more likely than Remploy employees to have been in receipt of QBs immediately prior to starting their current job. This was particularly true in the case of IVB and – among SEA employees – SDA.

As noted above, several people who reported having received Income Support before starting their current job did not tell us whether or not they were also receiving the disability premium. This also applies to receipt of the disability premium with both Housing Benefit and Council Tax Benefit. Considering the findings from the follow-up interviews which indicate that people are often unsure about exactly what benefits they receive (see Section 5.2), it is fairly safe to assume that many of this group did in fact receive a premium. This also has implications for analysis of eligibility for DWA which are also discussed further below.

---

1. These figures do not round to 14 per cent as a few people received more than one benefit.

Benefit received	Remploy (%)	Workshops (%)	SEAs (%)	All (%)
IVB/IB	3	12	10	9
SDA	0	1	7	4
Income Support	19	12	28	21
ISdp	2	0	4	2
Council Tax Benefit	3	11	8	8
Council Tax Benefit with disability premium	0	7	1	3
Housing Benefit	5	11	5	7
Housing Benefit with disability premium	0	4	1	1
No QBs	67	58	50	56
Don't know/missing	5	5	5	5
(Base)	(58)	(81)	(131)	(270)

3.6 Employment status prior to starting current job

Seventy-four respondents (24 per cent) said that they had been working immediately before starting their current job, 192 (71 per cent) had not been working and the remaining five per cent did not answer.

Of the 74 respondents who were working immediately before starting their current job:

- five had been working for less than eight weeks

- four for eight weeks but less than three months

- nine for three months but less than one year

- 15 for one year but less than two years

- 40 for two years or more

- one respondent did not specify the length of time they had been working.

Of the 192 respondents who were not working:

- 14 had been unemployed for less than three weeks

- 12 for eight weeks but less than three months

- 26 for three months but less than one year

- 40 for one year but less than two years

- 86 for two years or more

- 14 did not specify the length of time they had been out of work.

SEA employees were more likely to have been working immediately before starting their current job than sheltered workshop employees. This group was also more likely to have been working for a longer period in their previous job (see Table 14). At first sight, this finding appears to be at odds with earlier findings which suggest significantly longer periods of employment for sheltered workshop employees. However, the most likely explanation is that, for many people working in sheltered workshops, their current job is either the only one they have ever had, or the only one for many years. Table 15 shows that, for all respondents who were unemployed prior to starting their current job, the vast majority were long-term unemployed.

Table 14 Length of time in previous job

Length of time	Remploy (%)	Workshops (%)	SEAs (%)	All (%)
Less than 8 weeks	5	3	0	2
8 weeks to 3 months	2	1	2	2
3 months to 1 year	2	4	4	3
1 to 2 years	7	3	7	6
2 years or more	5	7	24	15
Missing/not applicable	79	82	63	72
(Base)	(58)	(81)	(131)	(270)

Table 15 Length of time unemployed before current job

Length of time	Remploy (%)	Workshops (%)	SEAs (%)	All (%)
Less than 8 weeks	3	7	5	5
8 weeks to 3 months	7	3	5	4
3 months to 1 year	16	7	8	10
1 to 2 years	14	19	13	15
2 years or more	26	48	24	32
Missing/not applicable	34	16	45	34
(Base)	(58)	(81)	(131)	(270)

3.7 Composition of respondents' households

Fifty-six of the 270 respondents (21 per cent) reported that they were currently living with a partner, husband or wife. Of these, just under 60 per cent said that their partners were working in paid jobs, while just under 20 per cent said that their partners were looking after family or home. In most other cases, respondents' partners were reported to be sick or disabled.

The details of respondents' household circumstances were similar across the three groups in the sample. The only slight exception to this related to SEA employees who, although less likely to have a partner, were more likely to report that their partners were working in paid employment (see Tables 16 and 17).

Forty-one respondents (15 per cent) said that they had children and, of these, 40 per cent reported that their children were currently living with them. Eight per cent stated that they had children who were either of pre-school age, or 18 years old or less and in full-time education.

There were some noticeable differences between different groups in the sample, with 36 per cent and 18 per cent of those working in Remploy and local authority/voluntary sector workshops having children, compared to less than 10 per cent of SEA employees. This is consistent with the younger age range of SEA employees and the fact that they were also less likely to be living with a partner than people working in sheltered workshops.

Table 16   Respondents' household circumstances

Living arrangements	Remploy (%)	Workshops (%)	SEAs (%)	All (%)
Living with partner	34	23	12	21
Not living with partner	66	77	88	79
(Base)	(58)	(78)	(118)	(254)

Missing cases = 16

Table 17   Partners' current employment status

Work status	Remploy (%)	Workshops (%)	SEAs (%)	All (%)
Working in paid job	55	59	65	59
Not working but looking for work	4	6	0	4
Training/education	0	0	0	0
Sick or disabled	14	0	12	9
Looking after home/family	9	29	18	18
Retired	14	6	6	9
Other	4	0	0	2
(Base)	(22)	(17)	(17)	(56)

Missing cases/not applicable = 214

3.8 Household income/
partners' benefits

Of the 56 respondents who were living with a partner, 49 gave details of their partners' incomes. Of these, almost half (45 per cent) had a net weekly income of less than £50 while a similar proportion had an income of between £50 and £150.

Among the sample as a whole, partners' median weekly income was £89.30. This figure was fairly consistent across the different groups in the sample, although slightly below average for partners of SEA employees (see Table 18).[2]

Table 18 Partners' average weekly take home pay

Weekly take home pay	Remploy	Workshops	SEAs	All
	(%)	(%)	(%)	(%)
Less than £50	47	44	43	45
£50 to less than £100	5	13	14	10
£100 to less than £150	37	31	21	31
Over £150	11	13	21	14
(Base)	*(19)*	*(16)*	*(14)*	*(49)*
Median	*£88.00*	*£92.15*	*£75.50*	*£89.30*

Missing cases/not applicable= 221

3.9 Household savings Just under two-thirds of respondents reported details of personal savings. Of these, 10 per cent reported having no savings, while just over one-third reported savings of £3,000 or less. Of the remainder, very few (three per cent) reported having savings in excess of £16,000.

There was very little difference in the amounts of personal savings reported by different groups in the sample, although a slightly higher proportion of Remploy employees reported having no savings at all (see Table 19).

Table 19   Amount of personal savings

Savings	Remploy	Workshops	SEAs	All
	(%)	(%)	(%)	(%)
No savings	16	6	9	10
£1 to £3,000	22	46	34	35
£3,001 to £8,000	10	11	17	14
£8,001 to £16,000	3	4	2	3
More than £16,000	2	3	3	3
Did not answer	47	31	36	36
(Base)	*(58)*	*(81)*	*(131)*	*(270)*

---

2. The number of respondents reporting their partner's weekly take home pay is higher than the number who said that their partners were working in paid employment. This may be because: a) responses to the question on earnings include partners' income from other sources (e.g. pensions or benefits); b) some respondents may have answered the question on partners' employment status incorrectly (e.g. where partners were in part-time work and receiving benefits); or c) a combination of these two reasons.

3.10 Eligibility for DWA

Analysis of the audit data has allowed us to estimate how many disabled people working in supported employment may be eligible for DWA. The analysis has been carried out in three parts.

3.10.1 How the data has been analysed

First, we estimated how many respondents – on the basis of the information provided on the audit questionnaires – were *potentially eligible* for DWA. By *potentially eligible*, we mean that respondents should meet the relevant qualifying criteria (i.e. receipt of QBs, working 16 hours or more, and personal savings within the permitted range). The estimation of potential eligibility has not, however, taken into account the level of employees' earnings which would of course determine their *actual eligibility* for DWA.

Second, using the data on income, savings and household circumstances we have calculated the level of benefit which those who were potentially eligible for DWA would be entitled to.

This part of the analysis allows us to estimate:

- how many disabled people working in supported employment are actually eligible for DWA but not claiming the benefit

- the amount of benefit they would be likely to receive if they did claim DWA

- for those who are not eligible to claim, the amount by which their earnings take them over the limit for the benefit at current income thresholds.

Third, we have examined the potential impact on eligibility of altering different elements of the qualifying criteria. In particular, we have examined the extent to which eligibility might be extended by:

- relaxing the requirement to work for a minimum of 16 hours per week

- relaxing the requirement to have been in receipt of QBs during the eight weeks prior to claiming DWA

- changes in the income thresholds.

The effect of each of these changes was examined sequentially. In other words, each parameter of the qualifying criteria was removed from the calculations in turn so that we could examine how many more people would be eligible as each of the criteria were relaxed. In addition we also examined the effect of relaxing the rules on receipt of QB's altogether. In this case however the other eligibility criteria were held constant in order to test the relative effect of this change compared to the other changes included in the anlaysis.

Eligibility and, where applicable, the estimated amounts of DWA respondents would receive were tested on a case by case basis using a computer programme which we have written for Statistical Package for the Social Sciences (SPSS). The calculations take into account the changes to DWA introduced in April 1995. Where particular items of information required to carry out the calculations were missing we have used imputed values as follows:

- hours worked (median hours per week)

- level of savings (modal value – i.e. £1,000 to £3,000) unless the respondent specifically indicated that s/he had no savings at all[3]

- usual take home pay and – where applicable – partner's usual take home pay (median take home pay).

However, in the case of respondents who either failed to answer the questions on receipt of QBs, or omitted details of their household composition (e.g. number and/or ages of children), it was obviously not possible to estimate their eligibility for DWA. Similarly, where people reported that they received Income Support, Housing Benefit or Council Tax Benefit but omitted to say whether they also received a disability premium, we were not able to ascertain their eligibility unless they were also receiving other QBs. (Although there were very few respondents who received only one of these three benefits on their own.)

Consequently, it is important to note that the number of employees who are either potentially eligible, or who are eligible and not claiming, is quite possibly slightly higher than the figures presented below would suggest.

Another important caveat to the interpretation of findings from the eligibility audit is that the sample was deliberately selected in such a way as to maximise the chances of including people who might be eligible for DWA. In particular, it is important to bear in mind that – in comparison with the broader based sample of supported employment workers from the screening survey – the audit sample contained far fewer people working less than 16 hours a week and also had lower average earnings. Consequently it cannot be assumed that either the proportion of people who might be eligible for DWA, or the effects of different changes in the qualification criteria, would be the same among disabled people in sup-ported employment as a whole.

---

3. We also tested the effect of imputing a zero value on the assumption that: a) no-one had significant savings; and, b) the number of missing cases might make the savings data unreliable; however this did not make any significant difference to the results.

As noted above, 18 (eight per cent) of the sample were already receiving DWA at the time of the fieldwork. Analysis of potential eligibility among the remaining 252 respondents has identified a further 51 (20 per cent) who – on the basis of the information provided on the audit questionnaire – met the relevant qualifying criteria for DWA in terms of receipt of QBs, hours worked and level of savings. These respondents were, therefore, classified as potentially eligible for DWA (see Table 20).

There were some noticeable differences in the level of potential eligibility for DWA among the different groups within the sample. In particular, respondents working in local authority or voluntary agency sheltered workshops were more than twice as likely to be potentially eligible for DWA compared to SEA employees. They were also more than three times as likely to be potentially eligible compared to respondents working in workshops run by Remploy. These differences are consistent with the findings presented earlier which indicate that respondents working in local authority or voluntary agency sheltered workshops were more likely to be in receipt of one or more QBs.

Table 20   Potential eligibility for DWA (existing qualifying criteria)

Eligibility status	Remploy	Workshops	SEAs	All
	(%)	(%)	(%)	(%)
Potentially eligible for DWA	10	36	15	20
Not eligible/unable to calculate eligibility	90	64	85	80
(Base)	(58)	(78)	(116)	(252)

3.11 Factors influencing potential eligibility for DWA

As noted earlier, the analysis included additional calculations to estimate the potential impact on eligibility of changing different elements of the qualification criteria.

The first factor examined was the requirement that employees should be working for at least 16 hours per week. We found that, although relaxing this requirement would slightly increase the number of Remploy and SEA employees classified as potentially eligible for DWA, the overall impact of such a change would be minimal as so few respondents work less than 16 hours in any case. Among the sample as a whole, omitting this requirement from the calculations increases the proportion of those classified as potentially eligible by only two per cent – that is, from 20 per cent to 22 per cent (see Table 21).

However, it is worth re-emphasising that the audit sample contained a much smaller proportion of people working less than 16 hours a week than the broader based sample from the screening survey (three per cent compared with 22 per cent). Consequently relaxing the requirement to work at least 16 hours a week might have a greater impact among people in supported employment as a whole.

We have also examined the effect of relaxing the rules on receipt of QBs during the eight weeks prior to starting their current job for those who do not receive any current QBs. Again, although this would bring slightly more people into the potentially eligible category, the overall impact is quite small – an increase of no more than three per cent (see Table 22).

In addition we have examined the potential effect of relaxing the rules on QBs altogether. This was tested by holding all of the other eligibility criteria constant while removing receipt of any QBs from the equation. Not surprisingly, relaxing the rules on QBs has a much greater impact than the other changes we have examined. Introducing this change into the calculation of potential eligibility produces an increase of almost 40 per cent in the number of respondents classified as potentially eligible for DWA (57 per cent compared to 20 per cent under the existing qualification rules). This increase in potential eligibility would be greatest among SEA and Remploy employees (see Table 23). Again, this is consistent with the earlier findings which indicate that both of these groups were less likely to be receiving QBs than those working in local authority or voluntary agency workshops.

Table 21 Potential eligibility for DWA (minimum 16 hours rule relaxed)

Eligibility status	Remploy	Workshops	SEAs	All
	(%)	(%)	(%)	(%)
Potentially eligible for DWA	12	36	17	22
Not eligible/unable to calculate eligibility	88	64	83	78
(Base)	(58)	(78)	(116)	(252)

Table 22 Potential eligibility for DWA (eight week rule relaxed)

Eligibility status	Remploy	Workshops	SEAs	All
	(%)	(%)	(%)	(%)
Potentially eligible for DWA	12	41	16	23
Not eligible/unable to calculate eligibility	88	59	84	77
(Base)	(58)	(78)	(116)	(252)

Table 23 Potential eligibility for DWA (all QBs rules relaxed)

Eligibility status	Remploy	Workshops	SEAs	All
	(%)	(%)	(%)	(%)
Potentially eligible for DWA	50	65	55	57
Not eligible/unable to calculate eligibility	50	35	45	43
(Base)	(58)	(78)	(116)	(252)

3.12 How many are
eligible for DWA but
not currently claiming?

Among the 51 respondents classified as potentially eligible for DWA, 20 (46 per cent) were found to be eligible for benefit but not claiming. There were also seven cases for whom entitlement could not be calculated so it is possible that the proportion of eligible non-recipients might be slightly higher than the figure reported here.

This means that, among the sample as a whole, eight per cent of workers in supported employment are eligible non-recipients and, added to the actual recipients, around 16 per cent could be getting DWA. The small sample size and the method by which it was selected means that we cannot gross up these proportions to the wider population of all workers in supported employment. Nevertheless, the findings clearly suggest that there are a significant minority who could be getting DWA but who are not claiming.

The incidence of people being eligible for DWA but not claiming was highest among workers in local authority/independent workshops and SEAs. This is because, compared to Remploy employees, more of these employees were in receipt of QBs and they also had lower average earnings. As noted earlier, SEA employees had the lowest average earnings of all. However, given their larger numbers and, in particular, the higher proportion receiving DLA, the greatest scope for increasing take-up of DWA is likely to be among employees in local authority/independent workshops. (This is also why we focused on this group more than the others in selecting people for inclusion in the follow-up interviews which are discussed in the next section of this report.)

The amounts of DWA which we estimate eligible non-recipients would be able to claim range from £1.77 to £61.28 per week. For just under 20 per cent of this group, the amount of benefit would be less than £10 per week. At the same time, over 10 per cent were found to be entitled to benefit of between £30 and £40 per week, while a further seven per cent would be entitled to £50 or more (see Table 24).

Table 24 also shows the amount by which those who are not eligible to claim have exceeded the current income thresholds for DWA. This indicates that over half of all respondents classified as potentially eligible had incomes which took them over the threshold at which they would taper off DWA.

However, in several cases the amount of excess income involved was fairly small (i.e. less than £10 per week). Consequently, we also examined the potential effect on eligibility of raising the current income thresholds by certain illustrative amounts. The results of this analysis suggest that, while raising the income thresholds for DWA would clearly have some impact on eligibility, this would not produce any particularly significant effect unless the threshold were increased by 20 per cent or more. Raising the income threshold by 10 or 15 per cent would produce an increase of no more than around five per cent in the number of people in our sample who would be able to claim. Raising the threshold by 25 per cent, on the other hand, would increase the proportion of those entitled to claim by 16 per cent (see Table 25).[4]

Table 24   Entitlement to DWA among potentially non–eligible and eligible employees

Estimated benefit entitlement	(N)	(%)
£20 or over	9	21
£10 to £19.99	4	9
£1 to £9.99	11	25
£0 to £9.99	8	18
£10 to £19.99	0	0
£20 to £29.99	4	9
£30 to £39.99	5	11
£40 to £49.99	0	0
£50 or over	3	7
Totals	44	100

Missing cases = 7

Table 25   Effect of changes in income thresholds on eligibility for DWA

Increase in income threshold:	Increase in eligibility (%)
10 per cent	1
15 per cent	6
20 per cent	12
25 per cent	16

Base = 44

3.14 Reasons for ineligibility   Although the findings from the eligibility audit point to a significant minority of eligible non-recipients, it is also clear that a large proportion of workers in supported employment are ineligible for DWA. Briefly, there are a number of reasons for ineligibility among this group.

---

4. We have also examined the estimated change in the amount of benefit people would receive if the income thresholds were raised. Again, the amounts involved would typically be fairly small, with most benefit amounts being increased by well below £10 per week even with a 25 per cent increase in the income threshold.

First, many had been in work for a considerable time. Consequently, if they are not receiving DLA they will not be eligible for DWA unless they left employment, received one of the other QBs, found work again and then claimed DWA within eight weeks. However, in practice, almost a quarter of the sample had been working immediately before starting their current job, and so would not meet the eight week qualifying rule.

Second, only a small proportion (less than 15 per cent) had been in receipt of QBs before starting their current job in any case. The situation with current receipt of QBs is slightly more encouraging in terms of establishing eligibility as just over one-third of the respondents were receiving one or more QBs (mostly DLA) at the time of the survey. Nevertheless, relaxing the criteria on current receipt of QBs would only bring a further three per cent of the sample within the scope of the benefit. However, as we have already seen, relaxing the rules on QBs altogether would have a much greater impact on eligibility as this would produce an increase of almost 40 per cent in the number of people classified as potentially eligible for DWA. This clearly suggests that non-receipt of QBs is one of the most important reasons for ineligibility.

Third, the other main reason why some people may be ineligible for DWA is that they are earning too much to come within the scope of the benefit. Despite the relatively low earnings among the audit sample, over half of respondents classified as potentially eligible for DWA (i.e. those who met the eligibility criteria) had incomes that took them over the threshold at which they would taper off DWA. Nevertheless, the analysis also shows that, while raising the income thresholds for DWA would clearly have some impact on eligibility, this would not produce any particularly significant effect unless the threshold was increased by 20 per cent or more.

Summary of Key Points
- Respondents had been working in their current job for an average of just under 6 years.

- The vast majority of respondents usually worked 16 hours a week or more, and only three per cent worked less than 16 hours a week.

- Nearly all respondents earned less than £150 a week. The median weekly earnings for the sample as a whole was £108 a week net.

- At the time of the fieldwork, just over one-third of respondents were receiving one or more QBs. Thirty-five per cent were receiving DLA, with only three per cent or less receiving any of the other QBs. Only 14 per cent had received QBs immediately before starting their current job.

- Eight per cent of respondents currently received DWA and a further six per cent had received DWA in the past, but were not currently doing so.

- Ten per cent of respondents who gave details of personal savings reported having no savings, while just over one-third reported savings of £3,000 or less. Of the remainder, very few reported having savings in excess of £16,000.

- In addition to the eight per cent of the sample who were already receiving DWA, a further eight per cent were classified as potentially eligible for DWA. Respondents working in local authority or voluntary agency sheltered workshops were more than twice as likely to be potentially eligible for DWA compared to SEA employees. They were also more than three times as likely to be potentially eligible compared to respondents working in workshops run by Remploy.

- The most important factors affecting eligibility were found to be receipt of QBs and the level of employees earnings. Relaxing the rules on QBs altogether would increase the number of people in the sample who are eligible for DWA by an estimated 40 per cent.

- Over half of all respondents classified as potentially eligible had incomes which took them over the threshold at which they would taper off DWA, although the analysis suggests that income thresholds would have to be raised by at least 20 per cent in order to have any substantial impact on eligibility.

- Other aspects of the qualification criteria did not have a significant effect on eligibility among this group. Relaxing the requirement that people should be working for at least 16 hours a week increased the proportion of those classified as potentially eligible by only two per cent (although this is also a function of the way in which the sample was selected to include larger proportions of people working over 16 hours). Relaxing the rules on receipt of QBs during the eight weeks prior to starting their current job (for those who do not receive any current QBs) only increased eligibility by a further one per cent.

- The amounts of DWA which we estimate eligible non-recipients would be able to claim range from £1.77 to £61.28 per week. For just under 20 per cent of this group, the amount of benefit would be less than £10 per week; over 10 per cent were entitled to benefit of between £30 and £40 per week; a further seven per cent would be entitled to £50 or more.

4 FINDINGS FROM GROUP DISCUSSIONS AND INTERVIEWS WITH EMPLOYEES

4.1 Aims and methodology

4.1.1 Objectives

The objective for this stage of the research was to examine attitudes towards DWA and any experiences of claiming the benefit among employees. Group and individual interviews were carried out at most of the case study sites with employees who, on the basis of the eligibility audit, were either eligible to claim DWA and were not doing so, or who had been in receipt of QBs but whose earnings were outside the scope of the benefit (with a cut-off point of £25 over the earnings threshold). At this stage we excluded one Remploy and one SEA site because they had no, or too few, eligible or potentially eligible employees.

4.1.2 Areas of investigation

The aim for the interviews was to investigate disabled workers' views on DWA, the reasons why some do not claim, and what measures might be useful for encouraging people to claim.

Key questions covered in the interviews included the following:

- Where do people usually go if they want to find out about benefits? Do they generally have any difficulties with claiming benefits?

- Is there awareness of DWA? Do they understand its role? Are the eligibility rules for claiming DWA understood?

- Is there awareness of how to claim DWA? Why are potential claimants not applying for DWA?

4.1.3 Approach to the survey

The areas of investigation outlined above were explored by two methods. Where a number of potential claimants worked in the same location, they were interviewed in a group. The method was informal; respondents were asked to discuss the topics freely and to exchange ideas, perceptions and experiences. Where a potential claimant had been identified in an isolated location, an individual interview was carried out using the same topic guide. All respondents were exposed to a DWA claim pack as a prompt. (Further details of the numbers and types of interview are given in Appendix 3.)

As well as obtaining the views of employees we were sometimes able to obtain the views of managers and staff where employees worked and employees' family members. The following report on this stage of the research utilises quotes from each of these sources to illustrate points made in the text.

4.2 Respondents' characteristics

The sample was comprised not only of individuals with a broad range of impairments but also covered a wide spectrum of individual experience and ability. Although there were respondents who talked knowledgeably and eloquently about their experience, there were others who were unable to contribute a great deal to the discussion because they had little understanding of, and/or knowledge about, benefits. In the words of one respondent:

> 'I don't know which ones [benefits] I get. They all look the same to me.'
>
> *(Group 2)*

Also included in the sample were a number of respondents (e.g. residents in a Mencap facility, respondents with severe brain injuries and/or limited verbal communication) who usually relied on others to organise all aspects of their financial affairs. Not surprisingly, therefore, experiences and perceptions of benefits in terms of claiming, understanding eligibility criteria, and the means of obtaining information were considerably varied.

4.3 Obtaining information about benefits

Respondents were asked where or to whom they would usually go to find out about benefits. The interviews showed that individuals rarely approach official agencies or others with general questions about their eligibility for benefits. Instead they would only make enquiries about a specific benefit, usually to the Benefits Agency.

There were many instances where there was limited knowledge of the range of benefits on offer. In a few cases, respondents (or their carers/helpers) had been visited by a social worker who had guided them through the range of benefits available; this was reported to have been of immense value to the individuals concerned. However, such contact does not appear to be continuous and, for the majority, knowledge of, and access to, information appeared to be limited:

> 'The onus is on us to poke around and find out.'
>
> *(Mencap home manager)*

> 'Really, there should be someone telling us to get benefits and that they are available to us. That's what should be happening really.'
>
> *(Group 1)*

> 'It seems that people don't get enough information about benefits.'
>
> *(Group 2)*

> 'I'm starting a group in Leatherhead for disabled people for the very reason that there's lots of things available for disabled people but they don't know about it, and also where to get the benefits and where to get the information...There's not anywhere that caters for it.'
>
> *(Group 1)*

Those who were able tended to look to leaflets in public places (e.g. the Post Office) or to media coverage for information. However, there were also instances of people hearing about the existence of a benefit to which they were entitled almost by accident. One respondent learned about the existence of DLA through his wife who was attending a day centre. Another was told about a benefit by a community nurse.

It was noticable that, overall, there was an expectation among respondents that someone would take on the responsibility of informing the individual disabled person about benefits which they might be eligible for. Many respondents were already in receipt of one or more benefits and felt that there should be automatic notification by the DSS of other benefits for which they might be eligible:

> 'We're all under a social services department, and they should inform us what our entitlements are.'
>
> *(Group 1)*

> 'It's all up to you as an individual isn't it, and it shouldn't be, should it?'
>
> *(Group 1)*

Respondents were more inclined to look to organisations (e.g. social services, disability organisations or sheltered workshops/SEAs) with whom they were already in contact in order to search out information on potential benefits. However, they often found that this information was not forthcoming. In the words of one respondent:

> 'This is the Queen Elizabeth Foundation for Disabled People. With that in their title, they should be telling us what is available for us. If we were talking about an independent company that's employing a disabled person, then you could turn round and say it's down to that person, but specifically for this company they should be telling us really what's available.'
>
> *(Group 1)*

Many respondents were dependent on members of their family to look for information on their behalf. Respondents were sometimes disinclined to discuss benefits with friends or work mates as this sometimes highlighted inequalities and lead to friction:

> 'We all get annoyed about what we can and we can't claim, so we don't talk about it.'
>
> *(ID # 6)*

Once a respondent was aware of the existence of a specific benefit, where would s/he go for further information? A high proportion of respondents stated that they would not know who to approach. Rather, they usually relied on a member of their family to enquire on their behalf or approached one of the key workers at their place of work:

'You can always go to the office because you know the people and the people know you. It's a big help.'

(Group 3)

Some respondents had approached the Benefits Agency, Citizen's Advice Bureau or their social worker for information and guidance. Only three respondents in the sample were aware of the availability of the Benefit Enquiry Line (BEL). There appears to be an unfulfilled need for informed advice which is combined with expert assistance. According to respondents, knowledge and willingness to help and explain is variable among Benefits Agency staff; also 'professionals' are not necessarily perceived as being sympathetic to individual needs. For example, respondents recounted instances of being handed a form to fill in without being given any advice or explanatory literature:

'I sometimes find that you meet people – in my own case with Housing Benefit, for instance… When I've claimed, you get different people telling you different things… They don't know as much about it as they should do, and you end up going to the Housing Advice Centre, and you end up getting the necessary advice from them. I've had to do that in the past to get it sorted out, so it can be a little bit of a battleground at times.'

(Group 2)

'That depends on who you are lucky enough to get. Some are helpful and some are awkward. They're not exactly rude, but it's their attitude, the way they go about things. They ask the same things.'

(ID # 5)

'Some couldn't care less but others are very helpful; it varies. There's a lot of them that don't have the knowledge. They just say – "Here's a form. Read it and fill it in."'

(ID # 3)

'I've gone off them [i.e. professional advisers] over the years because I don't find them helpful any more.'

(ID # 6)

In the case of two respondents, they had been advised by professionals that their decision to work was unwise. In their words:

'He was quite helpful, but there was something that did annoy me. He told me that I'd be better off not working. Who was he to tell me I'd be better off on the dole! Terrible!'

(ID # 4)

'When I applied for a job, the DRO [Disablement Resettlement Officer] telephoned me and said, "Oh, I wouldn't do it because you'll lose all your benefits." She said, "Stay at home and claim SDA." For a DRO I didn't think that was very good advice. I thought that was rubbish. I think she had the

<u>47</u>

attitude that because I was disabled, I was entitled to stay at home and claim more money and get bored stiff.'

(ID # 6)

4.4 The process of claiming benefits

There was a widespread perception among the people we interviewed that establishing eligibility and qualifying for benefits is a long, complicated and difficult process. As discussed above, reliable information is not necessarily available and what information there is is often hard to obtain. The DWA application forms and explanatory literature were perceived as being laden with jargon and language which is hard to understand, and this is exacerbated by the length and complexity of the forms:

'If you send for a claim form, it isn't just a form, it's a booklet isn't it — that you have to fill in. One question contradicts another, so in the end, you have to get on the phone to whoever has sent you this form to ask how to fill it in, else it'll come back.'

(ID # 2)

'The forms aren't clear. They use sentences or words that nobody understands. They themselves may understand it, but to somebody else, it's not always clear.'

(Group 3)

According to some respondents, many questions on the form probe intensely personal areas,[5] require the applicant to evaluate their own lifestyle in a totally unfamiliar way, and sometimes appear to be insensitive to the nature of their impairments. Moreover, some people felt that the form included questions intended to 'trap' the claimant:

'If you look at some of the questions, they have two meanings, and you've got to be careful how you answer it. It's like being in court; if you answer it wrong you're in dead trouble.'

(Group 1)

The overall perception was that the claiming process is designed to prevent success in claiming. A number of respondents backed-up this perception by describing their own experiences of claim benefits and being turned down. Some felt that it was only through persistence over a considerable period of time that they had been successful and received a benefit to which they believe they had been entitled to all along:

---

5. It is only on second claims that the DWA form asks about the nature of people's impairment in any detail. It is quite possible that the comments referred to above were influenced by people's experiences and perceptions of other claim forms (particularly for DLA). However, as they did not make this distinction during the interviews, this is not entirely clear.

'I've tried to get Disability Allowance for four years, and I did have help from Bob and Cynthia [key workers]. I got it backdated but it took me three or four years to get that.'

(Group 2)

Some respondents stated that they were reluctant to try claiming DWA because of these previous disappointments which led to them to believe that their claim would be rejected automatically:

'I don't know if I can claim anything but every time I get in touch with them, they say, "Oh, no, you can't have that." When we first moved here nine years ago, I applied for something three times.'

(ID # 6)

It was clear, therefore, that respondents found claiming benefits a considerable challenge. How would they like to see the situation simplified and made easier?

First, the measures in place to facilitate the provision of information (e.g. BEL and telephone help lines) were not available to some respondents because they were not able to use a telephone. Others who might benefit from these sources of advice and information often did not appear to have been aware of their availability.

Second, those who were not able to act on their own behalf were dependent on relatives, guardians, social workers or management at their place of work. These findings suggest that it is these individuals who should be targeted with information about the availability of, and criteria for, different benefits, including DWA.

Third, all respondents stated that they were more comfortable dealing with someone who knew them personally. This often meant that the burden would fall, in the first instance, on staff and managers where they worked. On the whole, respondents did not feel that these key workers necessarily had the time or the expertise to advise them, although they did acknowledge that they were usually at least willing to try. In the words of one respondent:

'We go to the office and they help us to fill in the form because if you go to Social Security, they don't help you. They want you to do it yourself. If we have a problem with filling the form we get help from work.'

(Group 3)

Fourth, ideally, respondents would like to see a body specifically set up to advise disabled people about benefits:

'It would be easier if you could get all the information you need from one source instead of having to go to different places.'

(Group 2)

According to respondents, this body would:

- inform disabled people or their advisers of the benefits available to them

- visit places of employment and explain the various benefits

- answer questions and help people to complete claim forms.

4.5 Awareness of DWA

Less than a third of the respondents recalled ever having heard about DWA. In addition, those who were unaware of the benefit included a home manager in a Mencap facility who was responsible for handling benefits for eight residents in his care. In his words:

'It hasn't been part of their portfolio. Is it a new benefit?'

(Mencap home manager)

For the majority of those who did have at least some awareness of DWA, this information had mostly been obtained via their employers. Managers at two sheltered workshops emphasised, prior to the group discussions, that they had made every effort to make their disabled employees aware of the availability of DWA. At one of these workshops awareness was higher than elsewhere and this was specifically attributed to information provided by managers. Managers added, however, that in a number of cases, respondents were unlikely to remember what they had been told and, overall, this proved to be the case. In addition, one respondent recalled reading about DWA in a specialist magazine, another in a local newspaper and one had heard about it on the 'In Touch' radio programme. Three respondents thought that they had been told about it by a social worker and two respondents recalled a television campaign about a year and a half previously. In the words of one respondent:

'I think basically if you wanted to claim Disabled Working Allowance it was like a top-up and you had to be doing over 16 hours. It was very brief though. It didn't tell you where to go or much information about it. It was just saying that it was the new government allowance that was coming out. I did apply for it but I was getting too much money.'

(Group 1)

Several respondents emphasised that they had not been exposed to information leaflets in places where they would expect to find them – e.g. post offices, public libraries, offices at work or in common rooms in residential facilities or day centres. Respondents reiterated their general complaint about dissemination of information about benefits. It was felt that, for people who are registered disabled, there should be automatic notification of potential eligibility for benefits such as DWA. The role of informing potential claimants is perceived as falling, principally, on the Benefits Agency, but several respondents also felt that there was an onus on other people and organisations like residential homes, disability organisations and key workers in sheltered workshops to take a role on this:

'*You brought the books to us, but where do people actually go to get them to start with?*'

(Group 1)

'*Unless you're a member of one of these magazines like 'Arthritis Now' you wouldn't hear about it. That's why I think there should be somebody in charge of disabled people. They've got enough medical records to know what you're able to do and what you're not able to do.*'

(Group 1)

'*As I'm getting Mobility Allowance I think they ought to notify you and let you know what other benefits you are entitled to and not just leave it to the person themselves.*'

(ID # 5)

'*They don't know what's available. They're not told what they'd be entitled to or could be entitled to.*'

(ID # 4)

It should also be noted that, in several instances, the interviews and discussions revealed a confusion between DWA and DLA. There were individuals in the sample who claimed awareness of DWA – indeed, some who stated that they had tried to claim DWA – who, as the discussion progressed, were clearly referring to DLA. Indeed, this confusion continued until detailed discussion of the DWA claim pack was under way. This confusion was attributable to the similarity in the title of the two benefits and a general lack of comprehension about the purpose of DWA (see below).

4.6 Understanding of the purpose of DWA

Nine respondents reported that they had applied for DWA but had been turned down. The general consensus was that they had not qualified because they were earning too much:

'*You can't get it! We've already applied, and we can't get it*'

(Group 3)

'*I was turned down before. I can't see me getting it now.*'

(ID # 4)

Approximately two-thirds of respondents reported that they had no knowledge of DWA at all. In order to facilitate further discussion of the benefit, prompt material in the form of the DWA claim pack was introduced. Prior to introduction of this prompt material, perceptions of the purpose of DWA ranged from total non-comprehension to a perception that it provided a subsidy for expenses incurred by going to work (e.g. travel expenses), or that it was a benefit aimed at part-time disabled workers:

> 'What is it about? What is it for?'
>
> *(ID # 2)*

> 'To me, Disabled Working Allowance is a benefit for people just doing a few hours a week because owing to their disability, they're unable to do full time. They just top it up to a more reasonable wage.'
>
> *(Group 1)*

> 'The people that did benefit from it were the part-timers really.'
>
> *(Group 1)*

> 'I think if you're working over 16 hours, you can't get it. I think – I can't remember.'
>
> *(ID # 4)*

Another view expressed was that it was a benefit designed to subsidise people who are more severely disabled. Hardly any of the respondents recognised DWA as a benefit designed to supplement earnings and encourage people to move into, or remain in, work. In the words of one respondent:

> 'I can get about. I can come to work. I have to come to work because my husband's disabled, but I'm 64 in February, and as long as I can come to work, I'll work, but I don't know anything about this Disabled Working Allowance. It wouldn't be of any use to us because we're of retiring age aren't we?'
>
> *(ID # 2)*

4.7 Reasons for not claiming DWA

4.7.1 Low awareness

As noted earlier, approximately two-thirds of the sample claimed that they had not previously heard of DWA. However, comments from some of the workshop managers suggest it is likely that a number of those who were not aware of DWA had been told about the benefit but had since forgotten:

> 'It's a start if people know about it – which they don't.'
>
> *(Group 1)*

> 'They don't know about it. It's not very well advertised is it? There should be leaflets in the Post Office actually. I've not seen any.'
>
> *(Mother of male interviewee)*

Respondents reiterated that, in their situation, they felt that someone should inform them directly of the existence of the benefit:

'*As you know, I work for the Shaw Trust, and maybe something like a Disabled Work Benefit – the Shaw Trust, your key worker, should tell you it's about work.*'

(ID # 4)

'*If DWA was appropriate, I would have expected them to tell me about it.*'

(Mencap home manager)

'*I think they should inform those who are long-term sick to see if they could claim anything more.*'

(ID # 2)

'*The DSS know of disabled people – their names and addresses and things. I think it would be helpful if they sent them the whole lot, and you could read through and see what you think you could apply for and go from there… It would be a lot easier if they could tell you what you can claim and what you can't claim rather than having to find out for yourself. I don't know what allowances are about. There are so many, you just don't know whether you can claim or not.*'

(ID # 6)

'*Surely there's a responsibility on the Benefits agency to inform me if they can apply for certain things.*'

(Mencap home manager)

4.7.2 Previous experiences of claiming benefits

As discussed above, several respondents view claiming benefits with suspicion and caution. The claiming process is perceived as being a difficult area requiring assistance in completing forms and entailing a lengthy procedure, with the chance of being turned down. Consequently, respondents are unlikely to apply for a benefit unless they have some confidence that they might succeed in their application. Some asserted that they had indeed tried to claim DWA but their claims had been rejected. There were also respondents who had a history of having claims for other benefits rejected and consequently lacked the confidence to claim again:

'*I've tried three times to claim for something and they told me I can't claim it so I think, "Well, why bother?"*'

(ID # 6)

There were also a few who feared that a claim might jeopardise the benefits that they were already receiving:

'*Some people might lose money. It might affect their Housing Benefit and things like that. It's worrying.*'

(Group 1)

'*In some ways, what's the point of claiming it if they're going to have it back. It's all swings and roundabouts. People think, like I think, that any money that you claim, the Housing Benefit'll have it back.*'

(ID # 6)

The DWA claim pack was shown to all respondents as a prompt during the interviews. Apart from helping to guide the discussions, this also served as an introduction for people who had not heard about DWA. Some respondents with literacy problems found this less useful however. For the rest, while the situation was clearly artificial and respondents would normally have more time within their own environment to work their way through the pack at their leisure, it was nevertheless instructive to observe which sections were studied and which ignored. For example, only one respondent noticed the simple explanation of the benefit on the inside cover of the pack folder. In addition, the sheer volume of enclosures was sufficient to deter several respondents from addressing the pack at all:

> 'That's probably why so many people haven't claimed. Because they look at the form and think, "Oh, my goodness!" and they fold it up and put it in a drawer.'
>
> *(Group 1)*

> 'You see what I mean? All these forms!'
>
> *(ID # 4)*

> 'You don't know where to start – for a start!'
>
> *(Group 3)*

The majority of respondents immediately extracted the advice notes and proceeded to read them, while leaving the claim forms in the folder. They did not read the back page of the advice notes and therefore did not note the provision of advice telephone numbers and addresses. Many who did attempt to read through the advice notes found difficulty in understanding what they were reading:

> 'Could you give me a simplified version of this?'
>
> *(Mencap home manager)*

> 'This would be something I could understand when I ask someone who [sic] I think will know.'
>
> *(Group 3)*

> 'It's hard, I don't understand it. It's difficult.'
>
> *(Group 2)*

The examples of income and benefit set out in the advice notes on pages 10 and 11 of the claim pack were a particular source of confusion. Respondents interpreted the examples as definitions of eligibility; most were unable to find their own specific circumstances on the page or incorrectly interpreted examples as definitions of the earnings ceiling for eligibility. Respondents felt that they needed a clearer explanation of the benefit. In the words of a few respondents:

> 'None of these figures relate to anything that I deal with.'
>
> *(Mencap home manager)*

'I don't really understand it. There's so much here... I certainly don't understand all this. There are so many different amounts for different things; I'd have to study it all night.'

(ID # 6)

Some respondents felt that a maximum weekly wage should be specified so that each individual could immediately see whether they were likely to be eligible for the benefit:

'I understand that it's for people working on a low wage, but what I want to know is, what they call a low wage'.

(ID # 6)

'If they said to you, if you've got £120 a week or more coming in, then you don't qualify, then you could work it out. And do they mean wages coming in as well as his Disability Living Allowance, or... does it count when you're add-ing things together?'

(Mother of male interviewee)

Confusion was also generated by the emphasis on working 16 hours a week and the wage levels quoted as examples in the advice notes. Most respondents were generally working 35 hours or more and most were tak-ing home over £100 per week and therefore assumed that they would not be eligible for DWA:

'If you work 16 hours and five days, you qualify, but if you're working like we work – something like we work – 30-something hours, it isn't for us.'

(Group 3)

'I've got more than what they state here coming in. I've got more than £70 coming in.'

(ID # 5)

'We've got no chance. They're talking about if you earn less than £54.75 a week – well, we've got no chance. Everybody here gets more than that. You're wasting your time.'

(Group 2)

'We fit the criteria but it seems that we're earning too much money to qualify.'

(Group 2)

'Money coming in for a couple with no children – money coming in of £100; well, unless I'm out of touch, most people here must get about that.'

(Group 1)

'£70 for a single person. Well, that's out of the window isn't it! I have to pay £70 a week rent!'

(Group 1)

In general, therefore, the conclusion was that DWA was *'not for me'*. The general perception was that the benefit is designed for people with more severe levels of impairment, for part-time workers, or for people on extremely low wages:

> '*It's for people who are more severely disabled and are only working part-time.*'
>
> *(Group 3)*

> '*This sounds like now more like the situation I was in with my unemployment for quite a while when I was trying desperately, because of the situation I was in, to get a job — it was about three years to get here I was in and out of a job and was not well, and at times it seemed that I wasn't getting too much money at all at the end of the day... Probably something like this would have meant I would have ended up getting more at the end of the week, more than what my dole was.*'
>
> *(Group 3)*

> '*I think the Disabled Working Allowance is for disabled people who perhaps can't do a full day's work but will give them an incentive to work, rather than full-time employment on a low wage. So someone doing 16 hours could get a top-up.*'
>
> *(Group 1)*

After exposure to the claim pack, a few respondents (five or six) felt that it might be worthwhile finding out more about DWA although the general view was that considerable assistance would be required if they decided to go ahead and complete a claim form:

> '*If I'm entitled to this, I'd definitely like to go for it, because every little helps.*'
>
> *(ID # 1)*

> '*It's them that write the damn things in the first place. They write them so complicated that you can't understand it, so you have to take it back to them. I suppose they're the best people to fill it in going on the information you tell them.*'
>
> *(ID # 6)*

The findings from the interviews clearly illustrate that there is a general lack of awareness about DWA amongst disabled people in supported employment which, combined with the perceived complexity of the benefit, presents a significant obstacle to increasing take-up.

In the final part of the report we consider some of the wider implications of these, and the other findings from the eligibility audit and interviews with key workers, and discuss some of the options for encouraging more people to claim.

Summary of Key Points

- Group and individual interviews were carried out with disabled workers who, based on the eligibility audit, were either eligible to claim DWA and were not doing so, or who had been in receipt of QBs but whose earnings were outside the scope of the benefit.

- Experiences and perceptions of benefits in terms of claiming, understanding eligibility criteria, and the means of obtaining information were considerably varied. Most disabled workers had only a limited knowledge of the range of benefits available for disabled people.

- Less than a third of the respondents recalled ever having heard about DWA. For those who did have some awareness of DWA, this information had mostly been obtained via their employers.

- Perceptions of the purpose of DWA ranged from total non-comprehension to a view that it provided a subsidy for expenses incurred in going to work (e.g. travel expenses), or that it was a benefit aimed at part-time disabled workers and people who are more severely disabled. Hardly any of the respondents recognised DWA as a benefit designed to supplement earnings and encourage people to move into, or remain in, work.

- Access to advice and information about benefits also appeared to be limited for this group. Disabled workers rarely approached official agencies with general questions about their eligibility for benefits although some would make enquiries about a specific benefit, usually to the Benefits Agency. Very few were aware of the availability of the BEL.

- Disabled workers were more inclined to look to people and organisations (e.g. social workers, disability organisations, or key workers in sheltered workshops/SEAs) with whom they were already in contact in order to search out information on benefits which they might be able to claim.

- A number of reasons for not claiming DWA were identified including: low awareness of, and lack of understanding about, the benefit; difficulties in locating reliable sources of advice; people's previous experiences of claiming benefits and their lack of confidence in the chances of being able to claim successfully; the complexity of the claims process and, especially, the DWA claim forms and guidance notes; and a general perception that DWA does not apply to people working in supported employment.

- A number of suggestions were made for ways of making it easier for people to claim DWA. These included: improving access to, and publicity about, advice and information services such as Benefits Agency telephone help lines; targeting of information about DWA on relatives, guardians, social workers and key workers in sheltered workshops and SEAs; setting-up a body with specific responsibility for advising disabled people about benefits; and automatic notification of potential eligibility for registered disabled people and people receiving QBs.

- Participation in the interviews and group discussions had encouraged a few people to try to find out more about DWA, although they would still need access to advice and practical assistance in order to claim.

5 SUMMARY OF KEY ISSUES AND CONCLUSIONS

5.1 Key questions addressed by the study

This study has aimed to answer a number of questions about the take up of DWA amongst disabled people in supported employment.

First, we have examined a number of specific questions relating to eligibility for DWA: how many people in this group are eligible, or potentially eligible, for DWA; how many who are eligible actually receive the benefit; how many disabled people in supported employment are eligible non-recipients of DWA?

Second, we have also examined the reasons for non take-up of DWA focusing in particular on disabled people's perceptions of DWA, its potential advantages and disadvanatages, and the process of claiming the benefit.

Third, we have tried to identify strategies for encouraging take-up. Particular attention has been paid to the role of key workers – mainly factory managers, supervisors and placement officers – in supported employment. Specifically, we have examined: the kinds of support and advice they provide for disabled employees; their knowledge and understanding of DWA; and, most importantly, whether or not they could be used as a resource for increasing awareness and/or take-up of DWA among disabled employees and job-seekers.

Fourth, we have looked at the reasons for non-eligibility for DWA among people in supported employment and examined what would have to change to increase the numbers of people who are eligible for the benefit.

In this final part of the report we summarise the key findings relating to the questions outlined above and draw out some general conclusions about the potential for increasing take-up DWA amongst disabled people in supported employment. We have also attempted to place the findings from the various parts of the study in the context of the findings from the main DWA evaluation.

5.2 Take-up of DWA among disabled people in supported employment

The first key question which the research has addressed is how many people in supported employment are eligible for DWA. Closely related to this, we have also examined how many are eligible for DWA but not receiving it. The answers to both of these questions are of course dependent on a number of considerations relating to people's employment situation (particulary, their weekly earnings and hours); the benefits they receive; and their household circumstances.

As far as their employment situation is concerned, the findings from the study indicate that the majority of people in supported employment have earnings which would potentially bring them within the scope of DWA. Similarly, the majority also meet the criterion of working 16 hours a week or more.

Just over one-third of respondents in the eligibility audit were currently receiving one or more of the main QBs for DWA (i.e. DLA, IVB/IB, SDA, or ISdp). Only a small proportion (less than 15 per cent) had received one or more QBs immediately before starting their current job.

Around one in five people in the audit sample were living with a partner or spouse and, of these, around two-thirds had partners who were also working. Average partners' earnings were very similar to those reported by respondents themselves. The majority of people in the audit survey had either no savings or savings of between £1,000 and £3,000. Very few had savings at or above the level which would disqualify them from receiving DWA.

Eight per cent of the audit survey sample were currently receiving DWA and a further six per cent had received DWA in the past, but were not currently doing so. Among the remainder who were not already receiving DWA, a further 20 per cent were classified as potentially eligible for DWA (in terms of meeting the existing qualifying criteria).

Almost half of those classified as potentially eligible for DWA were found to be actually eligible for benefit but not claiming. This means that, among the sample as a whole, eight per cent of workers in supported employment are eligible non-recipients and, added to the actual recipients, around 16 per cent could be getting DWA. The small sample size and the method by which it was selected means that we cannot gross up these figures to provide an estimate of eligibility for DWA among workers in supported employment as a whole. Also, because we were unable to calculate eligibility for some of the cases with incomplete information about benefits or household circumstances, it is possible that the number who are potentially eligible is slightly higher than that indicated by the analysis. Nevertheless, the findings clearly suggest that there are a significant minority who could be getting DWA but who are not claiming.

The amounts of DWA which we estimate eligible non-recipients would be able to claim range from £1.77 to £61.28 per week. For just under 20 per cent of this group, the amount of benefit would be less than £10 per week while over 10 per cent would be entitled to benefit of between £30 and £40 per week.

Combining the figures for people currently receiving DWA with the number of eligible non-recipients also allows us to estimate the overall take-up rate for the audit sample at just over 47 per cent. Although this may be low compared to the take-up rates for other types of benefit, it is nevertheless noticeably higher than the figures from the main DWA evaluation which estimated a take-up rate of only around 20 per cent (Rowlingson and Berthoud, 1996).

People working in local authority/independent workshops were more than twice as likely to be potentially eligible for DWA compared to SEA employees. They were also more than three times as likely to be potentially eligible compared to Remploy employees.

Similarly, the proportion of eligible non-recipients was highest among workers in local authority/independent workshops and SEAs. This is because, compared to Remploy employees, more of these two groups were in receipt of QBs and they also had lower average earnings. As noted earlier, SEA employees had the lowest average earnings of all. However, given their larger numbers and, in particular, the higher proportion receiving DLA, the greatest scope for increasing take-up of DWA is likely to be among employees in local authority/independent workshops.

5.3 Reasons for non-take-up of DWA

In addition to trying to establish how many people are eligible for DWA but not claiming, the study has also examined the potential obstacles to take-up of the benefit among disabled people in supported employment. In particular, we have focused on the reasons why people who are eligible for DWA do not claim. For example, we have examined whether or not people are aware of the benefit and, if they are, whether or not they understand its purpose and the criteria for eligibility. We have also looked at the question of how people perceive the relative financial incentives associated with earnings and benefits.

The findings from the case study interviews and group discussions suggest a number of reasons why people were not claiming which are summarised below. The most important of these were: lack of awareness about the benefit; limited understanding of the purpose of DWA as an in-work benefit; and lack of understanding and/or misconceptions about how DWA might effect other benefits which people receive. For several people – particularly in sheltered workshops – the lack of detailed knowledge about DWA amongst staff was also a significant obstacle as they often did not have access to any other sources of help with claiming.

5.3.1 Lack of awareness about DWA

Around two-thirds of the disabled employees interviewed said they had never heard of DWA and, among the rest, there was only a very partial knowledge of what the benefit is for.

The findings from the interviews and group discussions also highlighted a number of interesting misconceptions about DWA. For example, some people thought that DWA was intended to be a subsidy for expenses incurred by going to work (e.g. travel expenses); others thought it was a benefit aimed at part-time disabled workers; while some were clearly confused about the difference between DWA and DLA. Another view expressed was that it was a benefit designed to subsidise people who are more severely disabled. However, hardly any of the respondents recognised DWA as a benefit designed to supplement earnings and encourage people to move into, or stay in, work.

The findings from the interviews also highlight that most people had only limited access to information about the availability of benefits generally. Awareness of existing information services such as the BEL was also very low.

5.3.2 The process of claiming benefits

The study has highlighted that many people working in supported employment find the process of claiming benefit complicated and difficult. For people with learning difficulties, in particular, the claims forms and explanatory leaflets are often inaccessible.

As a result people often feel that the benefits system is designed to prevent them from claiming successfully. For some, this perception had been reinforced by actual experience as they had been turned down for benefits (including DWA) which they believed they had been entitled to. In some cases this also led people automatically to assume that they would be turned down for DWA also.

5.3.3 Perceptions of financial incentives and disincentives

Earlier we suggested that concern about loss of other benefits and doubts about whether or not they would actually be better off on DWA were two of the possible reasons why some people do not claim DWA. The interviews and group discussions with employees do not throw very much light on this question however. First, although one or two respondents were specifically concerned about the possible impact of DWA on other benefits, most of the people interviewed had apparently never even considered this question. Second, most did not have sufficient knowledge of the benefit to make any kind of judgement about whether they would be better, or worse, off if they claimed DWA .

This lack of awareness can obviously have an effect on whether or not people are encouraged to claim DWA. In particular, for DWA to have an impact, people must be in a position to know at least something about how much they might be able to earn and still be entitled to benefit. Those who did have some knowledge of the benefit, however, tended to assume that DWA is only for people on very low wages. Consequently, with one or two exceptions, they had not necessarily given any thought to how DWA might effect their own financial circumstances.

This is also consistent with the findings from the main DWA evaluation which suggest that 'reservation wages' (i.e. the level of wages people are prepared to accept) among potential DWA claimants are generally within the DWA threshold – even though they generally underestimated the amount they might be able to earn while still being able to claim (Rowlingson and Berthoud, 1996).

5.3.4 The 'disabled' label and attachment to work

As noted above, the benefits-earning equation did not figure very prominently in disabled employees, views on the potential advantages or disadvantages of DWA, suggesting that other factors might be more important. One of these other factors is likely be the value which people place on work as a goal in itself. Some of the key workers in the case studies, for example, were concerned that DWA carried a 'disabled' label which might deter people from claiming; also, that some disabled people were reluctant to describe themselves as disabled, particularly after having achieved the new status which having a job gave them. Further, as we know from the general literature on disability, there are certain groups (e.g. people with sensory impairments) who do not consider themselves to be 'disabled people'. Consequently, they may automatically assume that, as a 'disability' benefit, DWA has no relevance to them.

Some respondents also pointed to the difficulties associated with trying to overcome the perceived stigma of receiving benefit. Obviously, this is not an issue which is in any way restricted to disabled people. Recent PSI research on Family Credit, for example, also found that few people *'were entirely comfortable with the idea of claiming income-related in-work benefits'* (McKay and Marsh, 1995, p. 2). However, it was felt to be particularly problematic for people in supported employment for whom the aim of working is often as much about 'coming off benefits' as it is about earning a wage.

5.4 The role of key workers in supported employment

There is quite a large variation in the extent to which staff in supported employment are willing or able to provide assistance with claims for benefits. In particular, while the majority of staff in the case study SEAs had a direct role in supporting employees and job-seekers as part of their usual work activity, staff in sheltered workshops worked in management positions which, primarily, involved administration and production rather than any formal employee support role.

All of the key workers interviewed had been called upon for help or advice about benefits, including DWA, at times. However, the degree to which this was a normal part of their activities varied considerably from site to site and between different members of staff in each organisation. In particular, there is a clear distinction between SEAs and workshops. While all of the key workers in SEAs reported that they do provide advice on benefits, this was noticeably less common amongst staff in the sheltered workshops.

However, it is important to note that, even where staff do provide advice about benefits, this is often only quite general advice and only a relatively small proportion of staff were able to offer the kind of detailed individual advice which people need in connection with claims for DWA. There was also a considerable degree of variation in levels of confidence amongst staff about their ability to provide accurate information and advice about DWA. Not surprisingly some were concerned about the potential consequences of giving people the wrong advice.

The case studies have also highlighted the importance of supported employment staff having contact with, and back-up from, other more specialist agencies such as local Benefits Agency offices, Citizens Advice Bureaux and disability organisations. Staff who did have access to these resources were generally more confident about their ability to help with benefits claims as they were able to refer to them if they had queries about individual cases which they could not handle alone. Once again, however, there was a noticeable difference between SEAs and sheltered workshops as staff in the latter tended to have far less contact with these outside agencies.

Most of the key workers in the case studies had access to DWA information and claiming packs. Views on the value of this information were quite mixed. The majority reported that the information had been useful, but with some qualification. In most cases, this was because, they felt that the information would be of more help to them if it was simpler and easier to understand. Less than half of the key workers had attended any training or briefing sessions on DWA and, again, views on the value of this training were quite varied and some did not find it to be any help at all.

Although several key workers expressed doubts about their ability to give detailed one-to-one assistance with DWA claims, it was noticeable that some probably had a better understanding of the benefit than they realised. In particular, key workers' overall grasp of the purpose of the benefit and who is likely to be eligible was reasonably accurate.

Nevertheless, the various limitations on their ability to provide individual help with DWA claims suggest that, if they are to have any role in increasing take-up of the benefit, key workers will need to have access to more information and expert assistance. The implications of this for overall strategies for increasing take-up are discussed further below.

5.5 Strategies for encouraging take-up

The study has considered what strategies could be employed to encourage more people in supported employment to claim DWA. In particular, we have focused on the role which key workers in supported employment might play in this and the kind of resources they would need to enable them to assist people with claiming.

There are two main dimensions to this question. The first of these is the kind of information and advice which disabled people need, and how they expect to access this. The second is the ways in which key workers operate and, particularly, how they relate to disabled employees and job-seekers.

As we already know from earlier research, a large proportion of people tend to approach informal advisers – including professionals whom they are already in contact with – for information and advice about benefits (Perkins, Roberts and Moore, 1991). Our findings also highlight that this is certainly true of people in supported employment. Several people we interviewed also emphasised that they were more comfortable dealing with someone who knew them personally and were reluctant to call on assistance from more formal sources like the Benefits Agency. The clear implications of these findings is that, in the first instance at least, it is informal advisers – including key workers – who need to be targeted with information about DWA.

The need to focus on informal rather than formal routes to information-giving is also confirmed by the ways in which people in supported employment expect to obtain information about benefits. In particular, there appears to an expectation that – as with employment advice – information should come to them, rather than their having to seek it out for themselves. Some employees, for example, suggested that people who might be eligible for DWA (e.g. DLA recipients) should be informed automatically and sent a claim form. Although there is some logic to this suggestion it is very unlikely that such a system would have any discernible impact on take-up as advisory assistance would still be required to help people work out whether or not they are eligible and, in many cases, to assist them with making a claim.

The extent to which people in supported employment rely on informal advisers clearly poses difficulties for developing strategies for encouraging take-up through the use of existing formal resources like local Benefits Agencies. This does not necessarily mean that such agencies do not have a role to play. What the findings do suggest however is that these agencies would need to take a more pro-active approach than that characterised by services such as the DWA help line.

The claiming process itself could also be made easier by redesigning the claim packs in more accessible formats. This would be particularly important for people with learning difficulties. Nevertheless, in our view, the scope for easing the claims process by this method alone is probably fairly limited as many people would still need some practical assistance.

As noted earlier, key workers in the case study sites were, for the most part, willing in principle to try and assist with encouraging take-up of DWA amongst disabled employees and job-seekers. The main obstacle to using key workers for this purpose would clearly be the lack of detailed knowledge about DWA and the effect this has on their ability to give reliable assistance on an individual basis. At the same time, it is also interesting to note that, despite their doubts about their ability to give advice on DWA, several key workers were already advising people about other benefits such as Mobility Allowance. Given that DWA is still relatively new, this suggests that some key workers at least might become more confident about advising on DWA as they become more used to the benefit. Further, the responses to specific questions about different aspects of DWA indicate that some of the workers probably had a better understanding of the benefit than they realised.

These findings from the interviews clearly indicate that, while key workers in supported employment organisations can be seen as a potential resource for increasing take-up of DWA, there would need to be greater incentives and support to enable them to realise this potential.

As with employees themselves, the most popular means of providing such support would be through personal contacts and on-site assistance (e.g. practical demonstration sessions) from organisations with expert knowledge about DWA. Clearly, this primarily points to the role of local Benefits Agencies, although there may also be scope for working through other organisations with which sheltered workshop and SEA staff have regular contact. For example, some of the key workers interviewed also suggested that the provision of information about DWA would be improved by better co-ordination between all of the employment related agencies – particularly DEAs and PACTs. This would not only help to increase understanding and knowledge about DWA, but would also have the advantage of enabling people to receive advice about DWA before making any decisions about entering employment.

5.6 Reasons for non-eligibility for DWA

The main focus for this study has been on the numbers of people in supported employment who might be eligible for DWA, the reasons why some people do not claim, and what might be done to encourage take-up. A related, but nevertheless distinct, issue relates to the reasons why some people are not eligible for DWA in the first place, and what changes to benefit might have an impact on increasing eligibility. The findings from the main DWA evaluation (Rowlingson and Berthoud, 1996) suggested two main reasons for non-eligibility for the benefit: failure to meet the eligibility criteria, and the levels of earnings among potential claimants. This section of the report discusses the relevance of these factors to people in supported employment.

5.6.1 Failure to meet the eligibility criteria

First, many disabled employees may have been in work for a considerable time. Consequently, if they are not already receiving DLA or one of the other current QBs they will not be eligible for DWA. According to the current qualifying criteria, people in this situation could become eligible for DWA only if they successfully claimed DLA or analogous benefits first, or if they left employment, received one of the other QBs, found work again and then claimed DWA within eight weeks.

The findings from this study clearly suggest that this obstacle to eligibility does apply to many people in supported employment. People in the eligibility audit sample had been working in their current job for an average of nearly six years and the majority had been working in their current job for two years or more. Almost a quarter of the sample had been working immediately before starting their current job, and so would not meet the eight-week qualifying rule. Further, only a small proportion of the sample (less than 15 per cent) had been in receipt of QBs immediately before starting their current job in any case.

This is consistent with the findings on the low rate of transition from long-term incapacity benefits to work from the main DWA evaluation which showed that – even amongst people in receipt of the main QBs – there had been very little movement off benefit during the survey period; rather, most had already been in work for some time and less than a quarter had received any of the main QBs prior to starting their current jobs (Rowlingson and Berthoud, 1996).

Nevertheless, this aspect of the qualification criteria does not appear, by itself, to represent the main obstacle to establishing eligibility, as relaxing the criteria on QBs during the eight-week qualifying period would bring only a further three per cent of our sample within the scope of the benefit.

Relaxing the rules on QBs altogether, however, would have a much greater impact. Our analysis indicates that this would produce an increase of almost 40 per cent in the number of people classified as potentially eligible for DWA.

Second, some employees may be working less than 16 hours a week and so may not be eligible for DWA. These people could become eligible for DWA if they increased their hours or if the eligibility rules were altered to bring people working under 16 hours into the scope of the benefit. Once again however this is not a particularly significant factor in determining eligibility amongst people in supported employment as the majority work more than 16 hours a week. In fact, among the sample for the eligibility audit the average was well in excess of the minimum for DWA, at 38 hours a week. Even among the much larger sample of SEA and local authority/independent workshop employees used for the screening survey only one in ten work less than 16 hours a week, while more than 70 per cent work over 30 hours (see Appendix 1).

5.6.2 The earnings
threshold
The other main reason why some people may be ineligible for DWA is
that they are earning too much to come within the scope of the benefit.
These people may become eligible if their earnings were reduced or if the
earnings thresholds for the benefit were increased.

The findings from this study clearly indicate that this is indeed a major
obstacle to eligibility for people in supported employment, despite
relatively low earnings.

As noted earlier, the sample selected for the eligibility audit deliberately
contained a disproportionate number of people with low earnings.
However, even amongst the larger sample from the screening survey almost
two-thirds of employees earned between £50 and £150, bringing them
within the potential range of DWA.

Despite these relatively low earnings, over half of respondents classified as
potentially eligible for DWA (i.e. those who met the eligibility criteria)
had incomes which took them over the threshold at which they would
taper off DWA. In several cases the amount of excess income involved was
fairly small (i.e. less than £10 per week).[6] Nevertheless, the analysis also
shows that, while raising the income thresholds for DWA would clearly
have some impact on eligibility, this would not produce any particularly
significant effect unless the threshold were increased by 20 per cent or
more.

5.6.3 Changes to DWA
which might have an impact
on eligibility
Although raising the income thresholds would have some impact on
increasing eligibility, the findings from this study make it clear that the
main obstacles to establishing eligibility are the rules on QBs. First, only a
relatively small proportion of people in our sample were in receipt of any
QBs prior to starting work. Second, the present rules on QBs seem to be
creating a disproportionate degree of difficulty in terms of establishing
entitlement to DWA — at least for people in supported employment. The
main change which might bring larger numbers of people within the
scope of DWA, therefore, would be to relax all or some of the
requirements relating to receipt of QBs.

---

6. As the data for this study was collected during the summer of 1995, it is too early to
assess the impact of the £10 allowance for people working over 30 hours a week
(introduced from July 1995). However, there will obviously be some benefit to people
who are already receiving DWA and, presumably, the allowance will also provide some
added incentive for eligible non-claimants. In addition, some people who were
previously outside the scope of DWA will 'float on' (i.e. become eligible) due to the
extra allowance.

The introduction of QBs for DWA was intended to provide a means of providing a check on eligibility other than simply passing a disability test. Although some form of check on eligibility might still be considered desirable (e.g. to ensure that the number of claimants can be kept within the predicted range for eligibility and take-up), the present arrangements are rather like using a hammer to crack a nut as such large numbers are made ineligible as a result. Relaxing these rules would bring only relatively small increases in the actual amounts of benefit received but would do so for a significant number of people. Consequently, this is another mechanism for increasing eligibility which could be considered as part of any future changes to DWA.

Whether or not relaxing the rules on QBs altogether would be either practical or desirable is an open question. However, some relaxation – extending the qualifying period to 12 months for example – could be tested on a pilot basis so that the impact on eligibility and take-up could be properly assessed.

5.7 Final conclusions

The findings from this study highlight the need for a more proactive approach, both to informing people about DWA, and to encouraging take-up. Although the findings indicate that most people in supported employment are ruled out of eligibility for DWA, there is also a significant minority who are eligible for the benefit but not claiming it. In view of this, any measures which can help to raise awareness and understanding about the purpose of DWA will undoubtedly be of some value in terms of increasing take-up.

REFERENCES

Berthoud, R., Lakey, J. and McKay, S. (1993) *The Economic Problems of Disabled People*, London, PSI

Dalgleish, M. (1991) 'Countering the labour market disadvantage of disability', in White, M. (ed.) *Unemployment and Public Policy in a Changing Labour Market*, London, PSI

DSS (1996) *Disability Working Allowance Quarterly Statistical Tables: January 1996*, London, HMSO

Gooding, C. (1995) 'Employment and disabled people: equal rights or positive action?', in Zarb. G. (ed.) *Removing Disabling Barriers*, London, PSI

McKay, S. and Marsh, A. (1995) *Why Didn't They Claim?: A Re-interview Study of Eligible Non-claimants of Family Credit*, London, PSI

Perkins, L., Roberts, S. and Moore, N. (1991) *Helping Clients Claim Their Benefits: The Information Needs of Informal Benefits Advisers,* London, PSI

Rowlingson, K. and Berthoud, R. (1996) *Disability, Benefits and Employment: Final Report on the DWA Evaluation,* London, DSS/PSI

Thornton, P. and Lunt, N. (1995) *Employment for Disabled People: Social Obligation or Individual Responsibility?*, York, SPRU

Selecting pilot case-study sites

For the pilot stage of the study we wanted to identify three case study sites: one Remploy; one local authority, voluntary, or independent sheltered workshop; and one supported employment agency. We wanted to base our selection of pilot case study sites on as much information as possible, and make informed decisions about the type and extent of variation between sheltered workshops and SEAs that should be covered by the study. The details of how the sites were selected are set out below.

Remploy

Remploy were able to supply centrally held information about employees of each Remploy workshop and a typical or average Remploy workshop was selected as pilot case study site from this information.

Types of impairments

The largest single impairment category was mental illness and stress-related illness (including learning difficulties), which accounted for approximately 35 to 40 per cent of all employees. (The categories were used by Remploy and were not the same as those shown in the ES annual reports on sheltered employment. This group roughly corresponded with the 'neurosis, psychosis, mental handicap' and 'organic nervous diseases including epilepsy' categories used by the ES, which accounted for 36 per cent of all employees in the 1994 annual statement.) This group of people tended to have lower than average attendance and outputs and, consequently, lower than average earnings making them a potential target group for DWA. Among other impairment groups, output and earnings levels tended to be randomly distributed.

Earnings

The average weekly earnings among the majority of employees was £147 plus bonuses (at 1994 rates). However, there are approximately 600 employees who did not have a performance grade and whose weekly earnings averaged £120. This group might also be potentially eligible for DWA.

Selection criteria

In order to ensure that Remploy factories selected as case study site were 'typical' or 'average' units, the following agreed selection criteria were applied to the initial sampling frame:

(i)   The geographical clustering of Remploy sites should be reflected in the selection of factories for inclusion in the study. (Remploy factories are clustered mainly around the traditional industrial areas of the North of England and South Wales.)

(ii)   Units with less than 60 or more than 80 employees (i.e. those with higher or lower than average numbers of employees) should be excluded. (The mean number of employees per factory was 72.5.)

(iii)   Age, gender or type of disabilities of disabled people in supported employment should not be considered for initial sampling purposes because there was little variation between the factories (although characteristics of employees at selected sites would be checked at an early stage and alternative sites would be selected in the event of any potential biasing factors).

(iv)   Provided there were no other biasing factors, factory units would be selected from within the manufacturing groups with the largest number of employees as these were considered to be the most representative of total activity. (The manufacturing groups with the largest number of factory units were Textiles, Packaging, Furniture, and Manufacturing Services – accounting for around three-quarters of the total Remploy workforce.) With the exception of Furniture, it was agreed that the Manufacturing group could be allowed to vary at random in the selection of sites. (Employees working in the Furniture group tended to have slightly higher bonuses.)

(vi)   Interwork employees should be excluded from the sampling frame as this group tended to have higher earnings and, although they were paid by Remploy, they were all placed with individual public and private sector employers. It would have been difficult to survey this group within the constraints of the research design for this project.

On this basis, 10 factories were identified as meeting the sampling criteria across the following four areas: four in the North/North-West/Yorks and Humberside; one in the Midlands; two in South Wales; and three in the South-East. After checking levels of average earnings and any possible biasing factors in particular factories, the final three were selected – one of the three was selected as a pilot case study site.

Local authority, independent and voluntary supported workshops and SEAs

We found that only a limited amount of information about local authority, voluntary or independent sheltered workshop was available from the ES – Sheltered Employment Procurement and Consultancy Service (SEPACS). Similarly, only names and addresses of supported employment agencies were available from AfSE which, at the time, was called the Association of Supported Employment Agencies (ASEA).

Because of this lack of detailed information, we decided to distribute a screening questionnaire to sheltered workshops and SEAs in three geographical areas in England – London and the South-East; the East Midlands; and the North-West – with the highest concentration of disabled people in supported employment. The questionnaires included questions about the number of disabled employees, type of work, age range, range of disabilities, length of employment, hours worked and average earnings. Agencies and workshops were encouraged to give at least 'best guess' responses.

A total of 205 questionnaires were distributed in February 1995 and reminders and duplicate questionnaires were sent to non-responders during March.

Selection criteria Apart from availability and willingness to participate, the research team suggested the following two criteria for selecting the remaining three SEA and three workshop case study sites:

a representativeness (i.e. how the characteristics of employees in particular SEAs and workshops compared with the overall profile of disabled people in supported employment)

b potential eligibility for DWA (i.e. hours worked by employees and level of average earnings in particular SEAs and workshops).

Following discussion with the DSS, it was agreed that the primary criteria for selecting case study sites would be potential eligibility for DWA. Following this, a short list of eligible SEAs and workshops was drawn up, and each was contacted to discuss participation in the study in more detail, particularly the administration of the DWA eligibility audit.

Fieldwork details Interviews were carried out in the three pilot case study sites between March and April 1995. In total, we interviewed seven respondents across these three sites:

- three in case study one (Remploy)

- one in case study two (voluntary sector workshop)

- three in case study three (supported employment agency).

Interviews with key workers in the remaining case study sites were carried out between July and September 1995 (see Appendix 2 for further details).

Each respondent was interviewed in depth. The interviewer worked from a topic guide which covered the following topics: workshop/agency details; personal details and main work duties; information and advice on money matters; information and advice and benefits; awareness of DWA; information, advice and support in claiming DWA; and attitudes towards DWA. All interviews were taped and transcripts were prepared from the tapes.

Results from screening survey of SEAs and sheltered workshops Although the primary purpose of the screening survey was to identify workshops and SEAs for inclusion in the case studies, the survey has also produced relevant data on almost 5,000 disabled people working in sheltered employment. This provided the research team with useful information on the potential eligibility for DWA among this group to supplement the more detailed findings from the case studies.

Table A1.1 shows the distribution of questionnaires and response by type of agency, workshop and region. Sixty-nine (34 per cent) of the 205 screening questionnaires sent to SEAs and workshops were returned; 28 of 50 questionnaires (56 per cent) sent to local authority, voluntary or independent workshops, and 41 of 155 questionnaires (26 per cent) sent to supported employment agencies were returned. There was some regional variation in the response rates: 30 per cent in London and the South-East, compared to 38 and 46 per cent in the North-West and East Midlands respectively. This was largely because of the large number of SEAs in the London and South-East region.

Of the 69 workshops and SEAs that responded to the postal screening exercise:

- 30 agreed to participate in the case studies if selected

- 17 requested more information before making a decision

- 11 specifically indicated that they were unwilling to participate (mostly due to time constraints)

- 11 did not return the contact form.

Table A1.1   Distribution of postal screening questionnaires by type of agency/workshop and region

	London/ South-East		North-West		East Midlands		Totals	
	Sent	Returned	Sent	Returned	Sent	Returned	Sent	Returned
SEAs	116	30	22	6	17	5	155	41
LA workshops	11	6	7	3	7	6	25	15
Voluntary workshops	7	3	5	4	2	0	14	7
Independent workshops	9	4	0	0	2	2	11	6
Totals	143	43	34	13	28	13	205	69

Number of employees   The postal screening exercise generated data on a total of 4,874 employees: 3,629 from supported employment agencies; 741 from local authority workshops; 192 from voluntary workshops; and 312 from independent workshops (a total of 1,225 from all workshops). SEAs had the largest number of employees on average (89). (This figure is distorted by one organisation with over 2,446 – by far the largest number recorded.) Voluntary workshops had the lowest number of employees on average (27) and the smallest number of employees in any single workshop or agency was one (see Table A1.2).

Table A1.2 Number of employees in SEAs and sheltered workshops

	Number of employees			
	Total	**Average**	**Minimum**	**Maximum**
SEAs	3,629	89	1	2,446
Local authority workshops	741	49	13	132
Voluntary workshops	192	27	10	77
Independent workshops	312	52	5	157
Total	4,874	71	1	2,246

Types of impairment   As Table A1.3 shows, by far the largest group across agencies and workshops were people with mental illness, learning difficulties or nervous disorders, with a greater proportion of SEA and voluntary workshop employees with such disabilities compared with local authority and independent workshop employees: more than two-thirds compared with only 41 per cent.

There were other noticeable differences. For example, workshop employees were more likely to have mobility problems or sensory impairments compared with SEA employees, and independent workshop employees were more likely to have head injuries, compared to employees in SEAs and other workshops.

Table A1.3 Types of impairment by SEAs and sheltered workshops

	Total		SEAs		Local authority workshops		Voluntary workshops		Independent workshops	
	(N)	**(%)**	**(N)**	**(%)**	**(N)**	**(%)**	**(N)**	**(%)**	**(N)**	**(%)**
Mental illness/ learning difficulties/ nervous disorders	3,071	63	2,513	69	301	41	130	68	127	41
Mobility impairment	868	18	591	16	171	23	28	15	78	25
Sensory impairment	394	8	219	6	107	14	19	10	49	16
Heart/respiratory/ digestive problems	91	2	36	1	46	6	6	3	3	1
Head injuries	85	2	50	1	13	2	2	1	20	6
Other/miscellaneous	388	8	31	6	103	14	20	10	34	11
(Base: all)	*(4,874)*	*(100)*	*(3,629)*	*(100)*	*(741)*	*(100)*	*(192)*	*(100)*	*(312)*	*(100)*

Age and gender   Among the sample as a whole, 66 per cent of employees were male and 34 per cent were female. Local authority and voluntary workshops had a slightly higher proportion of male employees than SEAs and independent workshops (see Table A1.4).

Slightly less than half of all employees were aged between 16 and 29, although this was largely because SEAs had a higher proportion of younger employees (aged 16 to 29) than the workshops: almost a half compared with around a quarter. Consequently, SEAs also have a noticeably lower proportion of older employees (aged 50 or over) than workshops (see Table A1.5).

Table A1.4   Gender of employees in SEAs and sheltered workshops

	Total		Male		Female	
	(N)	**(%)**	**(N)**	**(%)**	**(N)**	**(%)**
SEA's	3,629	100	2,404	66	1,225	34
Local authority workshops	741	100	556	75	185	25
Voluntary workshops	192	100	139	83	53	28
Independent workshops	312	100	205	66	107	34
(Base: all)	*(4,874)*	*(100)*	*(3,304)*	*(68)*	*(1,570)*	*(32)*

Table A1.5   Age of employees in SEAs and sheltered workshops

	Total		SEAs		Local authority workshops		Voluntary workshops		Independent workshops	
	(N)	**(%)**	**(N)**	**(%)**	**(N)**	**(%)**	**(N)**	**(%)**	**(N)**	**(%)**
16–29	2,014	41	1,685	46	191	26	47	24	91	29
30–39	1,398	29	1,027	28	225	30	57	30	89	29
40–49	854	18	576	16	169	22	37	19	72	23
50 or more	559	11	289	8	159	21	51	27	60	19
Missing	*49*	*1*	*52*	*1*	*(+3)*	*0*	*0*	*0*	*0*	*0*
(Base: all)	*(4,874)*	*(100)*	*(3,629)*	*(100)*	*(741)*	*(100)*	*(192)*	*(100)*	*(312)*	*(100)*

Factors affecting potential   As Table A1.6 shows, three-quarters of all employees had been in
eligibility for DWA   employment for one year or more. This proportion is highest among workshop employees (86 to 93 per cent) and lowest among SEA employees (76 per cent).

Only three per cent of all employees had been in employment for less than eight weeks. Although the questionnaire specifically asked respondents to exclude people on short-term job placements, we were aware that this

75

might include a small number of such cases in the SEA figures. We have checked this before the final selection of the case studies.

Table A1.6 Length of employment of employees in SEAs and sheltered workshops

	Total		SEAs		Local Authority workshops		Voluntary workshops		Independent workshops	
	(N)	(%)	(N)	(%)	(N)	(%)	(N)	(%)	(N)	(%)
Less than 8 weeks	153	3	143	4	4	1	6	3	0	0
8 weeks > 6 months	446	9	406	11	20	3	5	3	15	5
6 months > 1 year	504	10	437	12	30	4	8	4	29	9
1 year or more	3,487	72	2,359	65	687	93	173	90	268	86
Missing	*284*	*6*	*284*	*8*	*0*	*0*	*0*	*0*	*0*	*0*
(Base: all)	*(4,874)*	*(100)*	*(3,629)*	*(100)*	*(741)*	*(100)*	*(192)*	*(100)*	*(312)*	*(100)*

Table A1.7 shows that around one in ten of all employees worked less than 16 hours a week and would not, therefore, be eligible to claim DWA at present. Around one in six worked between 16 and 30 hours a week, while three-quarters worked 30 hours or more.

There were marked differences in hours worked between SEA employees and those working in local authority, voluntary and independent workshops. Thirteen per cent of SEA employees worked less than 16 hours a week, compared to under one per cent of all workshop employees. Conversely, between 94 and 98 per cent of workshop employees worked for 30 hours or more, compared to 63 per cent of SEA employees.

Table A1.7 Hours usually worked by employees in SEAs and sheltered workshops

	Total		SEAs		Local authority workshops		Voluntary workshops		Independent workshops	
	(N)	(%)	(N)	(%)	(N)	(%)	(N)	(%)	(N)	(%)
Less than 16 hours	528	11	521	13	0	0	0	0	1	0
16 to 20 hours	216	4	199	5	9	1	0	0	3	1
20 to 30 hours	556	11	507	14	33	4	3	2	8	3
30 hours or more	3,476	72	2,304	63	699	94	189	98	300	96
Missing data	*98*	*2*	*98*	*3*	*0*	*0*	*0*	*0*	*0*	*0*
(Base: all)	*(4,874)*	*(100)*	*(3,629)*	*(100)*	*(741)*	*(100)*	*(192)*	*(100)*	*(312)*	*(100)*

Table A1.8 shows the weekly wages usually earned by employees in SEAs and workshops. Around one in six of SEA employees earned less than £50 per week, compared to less than one per cent of all workshop employees. Among the sample as a whole, 63 per cent of employees earned between £50 and £150 a week, placing them within the target range for eligibility for DWA. This proportion was highest among voluntary workshop employees (95 per cent) and lowest among SEA employees (60 per cent).

Not surprisingly, weekly earnings are closely linked to the number of hours worked. At the same time, although the majority of all workshop employees work over 30 hours a week, there is some variation in the proportions earning over £150. In particular, only five per cent of those working in voluntary workshops earned this amount – despite the fact that almost all of them worked over 30 hours a week. This suggests that hourly pay rates are below average for this particular group of employees, although other factors might have an effect, for example, differences in the availability of overtime payments and bonuses.

Table A1.8. Weekly wages usually earned by employees in SEAs and sheltered workshops

| | Total | | SEAs | | Local authority workshops | | Voluntary workshops | | Independent workshops | |
	(N)	(%)	(N)	(%)	(N)	(%)	(N)	(%)	(N)	(%)
Less than £50	561	12	559	15	1	0	0	0	1	0
£50 > £100	881	18	791	22	42	6	34	18	14	4
£100 > £150	2,207	45	1,394	38	468	63	148	77	197	63
£150 or more	982	20	652	18	220	30	10	5	100	32
Missing data	243	5	233	6	10	1	0	0	0	0
(Base: all)	(4,874)	(100)	(3,629)	(100)	(741)	(100)	(192)	(100)	(312)	(100)

Identification key   SEA (A) = Supported Employment Agency, North-West

SEA (B) = Supported Employment Agency, East Midlands

SEA (C) = Supported Employment Agency, West Country

Remploy (A) = Remploy Sheltered Workshop, London

Remploy (B) = Remploy Sheltered Workshop, North-West

Remploy (C) = Remploy Sheltered Workshop, North-West

VB Workshop (A) = Voluntary Body Sheltered Workshop, East Midlands

VB Workshop (B) = Voluntary Body Sheltered Workshop, South-East

#1 = staff member 1

#2 = staff member 2

#3 = staff member 3

#4 = staff member 4

Agency/workshop details

Name	Source of referrals	Number of employees	Proportion of employees moving into open employment
SEA (A) #1	• Social work teams /day centres	Around 30–35 at any given time	All end up with permanent jobs (although some will have had several placements first)
SEA (A) #2	• ES/PACT • Self-referrals	As above	As above
SEA (A) #3	• Social Services	As above	As above
SEA (B) #1	• Social workers	130	Nearly all
SEA (B) #2	• Social workers • DEAs	As above	As above
SEA (C) #1	• PACTs	300	Unable to give figures
SEA (C) #2	• DEAs • Social workers • Community psychiatric nurses • Self-referrals	As above	Unable to give figures
SEA (C) #3	• DEAs • Training providers • Self-referrals	As above	Unable to give figures
SEA (C) #4	• DEAs • Social services • Training providers • Self-referrals	As above	Unable to give figures
Remploy (A) #1	• Mostly from DEAs	Around 70	N/A
Remploy (A) #2	• As above	As above	N/A
Remploy (B)	• Mostly from DEAs	Around 70	N/A
Remploy (C)	• DEAs (some via Training for Work)	Around 60	N/A
VB Workshop (A) #1	• ES Jobcentres • Social services	60 (10 new employees per year)	N/A
VB Workshop (A) #2	• As above	As above	N/A
VB Workshop (B)	• DEAs • self-referrals (families)	Around 50	N/A

Support given to employees by agency/workshop staff

Name	Job title (staff)	Main duties
SEA (A) #1	Work Placement Officer	• Marketing employees to prospective employers • Vocational profiling/assessment • Work-related training
SEA (A) #2	Work Placement Officer	• As above, plus • Implementing and monitoring training programmes
SEA (A) #3	Work Placement Officer	• Research and development • Policy making
SEA (B) #1	Employment Consultant	• Job placement • Placement supervision • Management of agency staff
SEA (B) #2	Employment Consultant	• Job placement • Placement supervision • Management of agency staff
SEA (C) #1	Development Officer	• Job placement
SEA (C) #2	National Policy Co-ordinator	• Policy development • Evaluation • Information management
SEA (C) #3	Development Officer	• Job placement
SEA (C) #4	Development Officer	• Job placement
Remploy (A) #1	Factory Manager	• Dealing with customers • Financial management • Supervision
Remploy (A) #2	Office Supervisor	• Invoicing • Wages • Clerical work
Remploy (B)	Senior Supervisor	• Supervision of shop-floor activities
Remploy (C)	Factory Manager	• Managing production output
VB Workshop (A) #1	General Manager	• Marketing and finance • Liaison with Employment Department
VB Workshop (A) #2	Office Manager	• General administration • Employee welfare
VB Workshop (B)	Staff Manager	• Employee welfare • Co-ordinating Sheltered Placement Scheme places

Level of contact between employees and agency/workshop staff

Name	Type of contact			Frequency of contact with employees
	Vocational guidance	Workplace supervision	Job placements	
SEA (A) #1	Yes	No	Yes	Variable, but highest during initial assessment
SEA (A) #2	Yes	Yes	Yes	Varies from client to client and depending on length of placement
SEA (A) #3	No	No	Yes	Sees most clients two or three times a week
SEA (B) #1	Yes	Yes	Yes	Variable
SEA (B) #2	Yes	Yes	Yes	Variable
SEA (C) #1	Yes	Yes	Yes	Most monthly, but some employees seen only every few months
SEA (C) #2	No	No	No	Very little direct contact
SEA (C) #3	Yes	No	Yes	Regular contact until placed in job; as necessary after that
SEA (C) #4	Yes	No	Yes	Variable
Remploy (A) #1	Yes	Yes	Yes	Daily contact
Remploy (A) #2	No	No	No	Variable
Remploy (B)	Yes	Yes	No	Daily
Remploy (C)	No	Yes	No	Regular(?)
VB Workshop (A) #1	No	Yes	No	Daily
VB Workshop (A) #2	No	No	No	Once a week
VB Workshop (B)	Yes	Yes	Yes	Daily contact

Advice and support on benefits given to employees

Name	Do staff advise employees on benefits?	Type of advice/help given	Other sources of advice used
SEA (A) #1	Yes – but staff not very confident	• Help with claims forms • Advocacy • Advice on eligibility • Advice on entitlement	• Benefits Agency • Citizen's Advice Bureaux (CABx) • PACT
SEA (A) #2	Yes	• Personalised advice as part of vocational profile	• Benefits Agency • PACT • Other SEA staff
SEA (A) #3	Yes	• Personalised advice (e.g. calculation of benefits, advice on eligibility)	• Benefits Agency • CABx • PACT
SEA (B) #1	Yes	• Help with claims forms • One-to-one advice	• Benefits Agency • DWA helpline • Money Advice Unit (independent agency) • Also attends monthly 'benefits surgery' run by Benefits Agency staff
SEA (B) #2	Yes	• Help with claims forms • Advocacy	• Benefits Agency • DWA helpline • Social workers
SEA (C) #1	Yes	• Help with processing claims • Advice on eligibility	• Benefits Agency • DEAs • ES Jobcentres • CABx • Local Law Centre
SEA (C) #2	Yes (Agency staff, but not management)	• As above	• As above
SEA (C) #3	Yes, but concerned about possibility of giving incorrect advice	• Help with claims forms • General information on DWA	• Benefits Agency • CABx • (Also used to use ES, but found staff did not have sufficient in-depth knowledge)
SEA (C) #4	Yes, but concerned about possibility of giving incorrect advice	• Help with claims forms • General information on DWA	• Benefits Agency • CABx • Disability organisations

Advice and support on benefits given to employees (ctd)

Name	Do staff advise employees on benefits?	Type of advice/help given	Other sources of advice used
Remploy A #1	No: staff have limited knowledge of benefits; also, benefits considered to be employees' private business	• No help given other than general advice 'money matters' (e.g. how to open a bank account)	• PACT • Social Services • CABx • Disability organisations • Deaf Clubs
Remploy (A) #2	No: staff have limited knowledge of benefits	• N/A (Any assistance given is provided by Factory Manager only)	N/A
Remploy (B)	No: staff have limited knowledge of benefits	• No advice given, but will refer to other agencies	• CABx • DEAs
Remploy (C)	Yes: employees have access to advice from Personnel Officer, union representative, and Benefits Officer	• Aim to provide 'first point of contact' for benefits advice; also assists with form-filling, dealing with bank accounts, etc.	• Benefits Agency
VB Workshop (A) #1	Yes, but staff 'not experts'	• Help with filling-in claims forms	• CABx • Voluntary agencies
VB Workshop (A) #2	Yes	• Help with filling-in claims forms • Will initiate claims (mostly for DLA)	• Social services • DIAL • DEAs
VB Workshop (B)	No: staff do not have sufficient expertise	N/A (although staff will discuss benefits and refer as appropriate)	• DEAs • Social workers • CABx

Awareness about DWA amongst agency/workshop staff

Name	Information received	Views on information	Training received	Views on training
SEA (A) #1	Yes – DWA pack from DSS	Found information inaccessible	Yes	Very useful
SEA (A) #2	Yes – DWA pack from DSS	Quite useful	Yes	Did not fully understand content
SEA (A) #3	Yes – all published information, plus briefings from Benefits Agency	Quite useful, but found direct contact with Benefits Agency staff most help	Yes	Very useful
SEA (B) #1	Yes – from Benefits Agency	Yes	No	N/A
SEA (B) #2	Yes – DWA information pack from DSS	Very useful	No	N/A
SEA (C) #1	Yes – leaflets from Benefits Agency	Quite useful, but could be written more simply	No	N/A
SEA (C) #2	Yes – Freephone information (DSS)	No: problems with getting through; also with obtaining consistent advice	Yes	A useful starting point, but 'reality does not match up to DSS PR'
SEA (C) #3	Yes – leaflets and claims pack	Very 'user friendly'	Yes	Not very helpful
SEA (C) #4	Yes – Freephone information (DSS) and leaflets from Benefits Agency	Not detailed enough	No	N/A
Remploy (A) #1	Yes – DWA information pack from DSS; plus internal company briefings	Limited use as staff not engaged in benefits advice	No	N/A
Remploy (A) #2	No	N/A	No	N/A
Remploy (B)	No	N/A	No	N/A
Remploy (C)	Received DWA information pack via Personnel Dept, plus leaflets to distribute to employees	Useful for explaining the benefit; 'straightforward and easy to follow'	No	N/A

Awareness about DWA amongst agency/workshop staff (ctd)

Name	Information received	Views on information	Training received	Views on training
VB Workshop (A) #1	Yes – DWA information pack from DSS	Not useful because: a) too much documentation; b) raised expectations which could not be met	Yes	Not useful as staff felt no employees would be eligible
VB Workshop (A) #2	Yes – 'Guide to DWA' and booklet produced by County Council	Very useful	Yes	Quite useful
VB Workshop (B)	Yes – DWA pack from DSS plus information from DEAs	Has not used in practice	No	N/A

Level of involvement in DWA claims amongst agency/workshop staff

Name	Assists with claims for DWA	Knowledge of employees' circumstances	Other agencies employees referred to
SEA (A) #1	Generally not; often too busy	Yes	• Benefits Agency
SEA (A) #2	General advice only; although may help with first claim	Yes	• None
SEA (A) #3	Advice on eligibility; assistance with filling in claims forms; plus liaison with CABx or Benefits Agency	Yes	• CABx • Benefits Agency
SEA (B) #1	Yes: help with completing claims; contact with DWA helpline	Yes	• Benefits Agency • Money Advice Unit (independent agency)
SEA (B) #2	Yes: help with completing claims; personalised calculation of eligibility, entitlement and effect on other benefits (using software package in-house)	Yes	• Benefits Agency • DWA Helpline
SEA (C) #1	Yes: help with filling in forms plus general advice	Some employees only	• DEAs
SEA (C) #2	Yes: help with filling in forms plus telephone enquiries to DSS	Some employees only	• CABx
SEA (C) #3	Yes: help with filling in forms and attempts to assess suitability for DWA on an individual basis; refers clients to Benefits Agency if necessary	Yes	• Benefits Agency • CABx
SEA (C) #4	Yes: help with filling in forms and attempts to assess suitability for DWA on an individual basis	Yes	• Benefits Agency • Local advice centre • Advocacy workers
Remploy (A) #1	Not able to assist due to large number of employees	Partial knowledge only	• CABx • Adult Training Centres • PACT

Level of involvement in DWA claims amongst agency/workshop staff (ctd)

Name	Assists with claims for DWA	Knowledge of employees' circumstances	Other agencies employees referred to
Remploy (A) #2	None	No	None (but see above)
Remploy (B)	General advice only; staff do not have any DWA documentation	No: relevant information at site office, but not passed on to factory staff	• Benefits Agency (but mostly for Mobility Allowance claims)
Remploy (C)	Yes: helps to establish eligibility (although, in all cases to date, claims have not been pursued)	Yes: staff have details about employees benefits, rent, earnings, etc., but do not always have full details of household circumstances	• Benefits Agency
VB Workshop (A) #1	Assistance with filling in claims forms (although very few for DWA)	Some employees only	• CABx
VB Workshop (A) #2	Will provide assistance, but this is *not* seen as part of staff role (although very few for DWA)	Yes	• Social workers
VB Workshop (B)	Assistance with claims mostly provided by social workers	Some employees only	• Social workers • DEAs

Workshop/agency staff views on DWA eligibility criteria

Name	How many employees considered potentially eligible for DWA?	Views on why potentially eligible employees do not claim
SEA (A) #1	A 'significant' proportion	Jobs set up too quickly (i.e. not enough time to consider benefit implications)
SEA (A) #2	Some (unsure how many)	Most already working when DWA introduced
SEA (A) #3	Some (unsure how many)	SEA have only started considering DWA in last 12 months Some employees may have left it too late to claim
SEA (B) #1	None who have not claimed already	N/A
SEA (B) #2	None who have not claimed already	N/A
SEA (C) #1	'One or two' only	Benefits Agency staff seen as unapproachable
SEA (C) #2	Some (unsure how many)	Claims forms too complicated Employees 'too distracted' when starting a new job
SEA (C) #3	Some (unsure how many)	Employees not given adequate information on DWA by Jobcentres, Benefits Agency, or other professionals they come into contact with
SEA (C) #4	'A few' (seven or eight)	Some employees may have left it too late to claim Mistrust of the benefit system Benefit system inaccessible to people with learning difficulties
Remploy (A) #1	Around 10 to 15 per cent	DWA not given high enough priority by employers Employees' concerns about losing other benefits
Remploy (A) #2	Not asked (but see above)	N/A
Remploy (B)	Five or six (10 per cent) may be eligible	Employees do not know about DWA
Remploy (C)	Most employees thought to be earning too much for DWA	N/A

Workshop/agency staff views on DWA eligibility criteria (ctd)

Name	How many employees considered potentially eligible for DWA?	Views on why potentially eligible employees do not claim
VB Workshop (A) #1	Very few	Poor image of DWA
		Employees do not know about DWA
VB Workshop (A) #2	Possibly around five workers (10 per cent)	Don't know
VB Workshop (B)	Some (unsure how many)	Lack of awareness about DWA
		Claims forms too long/too complicated

Perceived advantages and disadvantages of DWA

Name	What are seen as main advantages of DWA?	What are seen as main disadvantages of DWA?
SEA (A) #1	• Can be an incentive to enter employment	• Many employees assume DWA not relevant to them
SEA (A) #2	• Two-year linking rule	• Earnings threshold too low • Complex application procedures • Potential conflict with SEA's aim to maximise clients' earnings
SEA (A) #3	• Two-year linking rule provides important 'safety net'	• Earnings threshold too low
SEA (B) #1	• Increases income	• Complex application procedures
SEA (B) #2	• Helps people to come off benefit and into work • Two-year linking rule	• Complex application procedures • Sixteen hours rule
SEA (C) #1	• Limited advantages	• Claims forms too complicated
SEA (C) #2	• Very useful benefit in theory, but still at the 'infant stage' with 'unrealised potential'	• Claims forms too complicated
SEA (C) #3	• 'Good value for money' (i.e. cost-effective alternative to unemployment) • Two-year linking rule	• Means testing (DWA should not take partners' income into account)
SEA (C) #4	• Enables people to work for low wages and still have a relatively reasonable income	• Could be seen as patronising • Little incentive to increase earnings or seek promotion for people on average wages
Remploy (A) #1	• Financial incentive for people on *very* low wages	• Little incentive to increase earnings or seek promotion for people on average wages • Concerns about being labelled as 'disabled'
Remploy (A) #2	• Useful to top up low wages	• Unable to say
Remploy (B)	• Useful to top up low wages (workshop has seen job applicants who were better off on benefits)	• Potential problems with overtime payments
Remploy (C)	• Useful for part-time employees	• Only applies to a small group of employees

Perceived advantages and disadvantages of DWA (ctd)

Name	What are seen as main advantages of DWA?	What are seen as main disadvantages of DWA?
VB Workshop (A) #1	• Little advantages to workshops' employees	• Eligibility rules 'far too complex'
VB Workshop (A) #2	• Little advantages to most employees	• Not very useful for full-time or single employees
		• Having to reapply every six months
VB Workshop (B)	• Increases income	• Requirement to have QBs

Views on barriers to take-up of DWA

Name	What are seen as main barriers to claiming DWA?	What measures would encourage take-up of DWA?
SEA (A) #1	• Concerns about losing other benefits • Earnings threshold too low • Lack of awareness about DWA among professional advisors	• Increased awareness about DWA amongst social workers, employment advisors, etc.
SEA (A) #2	• Complex claiming and reclaiming procedures (particular disincentive if moving in and out of employment) • Earnings threshold too low • Minimum 16 hours rule	• Extension of two-year protection to higher earners
SEA (A) #3	• Earnings threshold too low • Lack of information • Bad press in early months following Introduction of DWA • Minimum 16 hours rule	• Extension of two-year protection to higher earners • More information for professionals and families • Improved co-ordination between employment and benefit agencies
SEA (B) #1	• Minimum 16 hours rule • Lack of information • Perceived threat to other benefits (employees and parents) • Social stigma of 'disabled' label	• More targeted information • Practical presentations (by Benefits Agency) on DWA for potential claimants • Make qualifying criteria easier to understand • More privacy when discussing benefit and financial situation (with ES staff in particular)
SEA (B) #2	• Eligibility rules too restrictive • Perceived threat to other benefits	• More targeted information (e.g. for people with visual impairments) • Advertising (e.g. television/radio) to generate interest in DWA
SEA (C) #1	• Lack of understanding about the purpose of DWA • Stigma of being on benefits	• Simplify claims procedures • More effective publicity through television and popular (i.e. tabloid) press • Clearer information on how to claim and where to go for advice
SEA (C) #2	• Claims procedures too complex • Some employees already in employment for too long • People not well informed about purpose of DWA; consequently, do not see claiming as a priority	• A more proactive approach to encouraging take-up • Simplify claims form • Increase awareness of eligibility to counter employees assuming the benefit does not apply to them

Name	What are seen as main barriers to claiming DWA?	What measures would encourage take-up of DWA?
SEA (C) #3	• Some employees already in employment for too long • Lack of awareness about DWA • Perceived threat to existing benefits • Earnings threshold too low	• Allow claims to be made *before* starting work so that claimants can be sure of their overall benefit position • Target information at specialist organisations (e.g. SEAs) who work with disabled job-seekers
SEA (C) #4	• DWA very difficult to understand for people with learning difficulties • People with learning difficulties unlikely to have QBs like DLA • Families/parents may discourage people from working if dependent on benefits • Professionals do not know enough to encourage claiming; • Earnings threshold too low • Social stigma of 'disabled' label	• Use outreach Benefit Officers to raise awareness about DWA in further education colleges • Specialist DWA advisors in local Jobcentres or Benefits Agency offices • Target information in places where potential claimants are likely to be (e.g. special schools, Adult Training Centres) • Target information on people known to be receiving QBs
Remploy (A) #1	• Complexity of the benefit • Stigma and negative labelling • Effect on other benefits (both perceived and/or actual) • Restrictive rules on QBs • Poor understanding of the purpose of DWA (i.e. as an in-work benefit) means that many people automatically assume they cannot apply	• Simplification of assessment process so that employers can handle claims directly • Improved co-ordination with, and follow-up by, DEAs (i.e. DEAs should advise people about DWA before any decisions about starting work • Removal/relaxation of links to QBs • Increase earnings threshold to encourage career progression
Remploy (A) #2	• Earnings threshold too low	• Improve advice given to employees on how to claim
Remploy (B)	• Lack of knowledge about DWA • Inability to complete claims forms • Effect on other benefits	• More information (for staff and employees
Remploy (C)	• Most employees better-off on other benefits • Earnings threshold too low	• Change eligibility criteria (16 hours rule and earnings threshold in particular)
VB Workshop (A) #1	• Complexity of eligibility criteria • Risks associated with 'benefits trap' • Perceived effect on other benefits	• More targeted information (e.g. on DLA recipients) • Increase earnings threshold

Name	What are seen as main barriers to claiming DWA?	What measures would encourage take-up of DWA?
VB Workshop (A) #2	• Complexity of eligibility criteria • Lack of understanding about purpose of DWA • Effect on other benefits • Employees expectations that they will not qualify	• More targeted information • Increase earnings threshold • Simpler information with clear examples of eligibility criteria • Increase awareness about DWA amongst disabled people
VB Workshop (B)	• Illiteracy amongst workshop employees (consequently, claims forms are too complex and put people off claiming) • Rules on QBs	• Simplify claims forms • Increased awareness about DWA • Information to be provided through practical training rather than literature

APPENDIX 3 SAMPLE DETAILS FOR FOLLOW-UP INTERVIEWS WITH DISABLED EMPLOYEES

Group discussions

Group 1 Seven respondents, mixed sex; employed at a VB run sheltered workshop in the South East

Group 2 Six respondents, male; employed at a VB run sheltered workshop in the East Midlands

Group 3 Nine respondents, mixed sex; employed at a VB run sheltered workshop in the East Midlands

Individual interviews (ID No)

1 Male – employed by Remploy (sheltered workshop)

2 Female – employed by Remploy (sheltered workshop)

3 Female – employed by Remploy (sheltered workshop)

4 Male – interviewed at home (SEA client)

5 Male – employed by Remploy (sheltered workshop)

6 Female – interviewed at home (SEA client)

7 Male – interviewed at home (SEA client)

8 Female – interviewed at Mencap residential care home (SEA client)

9 Male – interviewed at Mencap residential care home (SEA client)

APPENDIX 4   QUESTIONNAIRES USED FOR SCREENING SURVEY AND ELIGIBILITY AUDIT

IN CONFIDENCE

REFERENCE NO.

DISABILITY WORKING ALLOWANCE AND SUPPORTED EMPLOYMENT

SCREENING QUESTIONNAIRE for LOCAL AUTHORITY, VOLUNTARY AGENCY and INDEPENDENT WORKSHOPS

A STUDY BY THE INDEPENDENT POLICY STUDIES INSTITUTE FOR THE DEPARTMENT OF SOCIAL SECURITY

Policy Studies Institute,
100 Park Village East,
LONDON NW1 3SR

Tel: 071 387 2171
Fax: 071 388 0914

COMPLETING THE QUESTIONNAIRE

Most questions asked you to give numbers or estimates, for example, the number of employees. If you cannot give an exact number, please give an estimate or your 'best guess'?

There are also some 'open-ended' questions. Again please write your response in the large boxes provided.

If you are unable to answer a question, please write 'Don't know' next to the box.

All information given will be treated in the strictest confidence.

If you have any queries, please contact GERRY ZARB or NIGEL JACKSON at the address below:

Policy Studies Institute,
100 Park Village East,
London NW1 3SR

Tel: 071 387 2171
Fax: 071 388 0914

Q1a. How many disabled employees do you currently employ?
(Please write in box)

TOTAL

b. How many of these are **male**?
(Please write in box)

MALE

c. How many of these are **female**?
(Please write in box)

FEMALE

Q2. What type, or types, of work are currently done by your disabled?
(**Please write a brief description in box**)

Q3. How many of your disabled employees are in each of the following age groups: (**Please write in box**)

NUMBER OF EMPLOYEES

a. 16 to 29

b. 30 to 39

c. 40 to 49

d. 50 and over

Q4. How many of your employees have: (Please write in boxes)

NUMBER OF EMPLOYEES

a. Learning difficulties/ mental handicaps/ nervous disorders

b. Mobility impairments including upper limb disorders relating to reaching, stretching, gripping or turning

c. Sensory impairments

d. Heart, respiratory & digestive problems

e. Head injuries

g. Other/miscellaneous

Q5. How many of your employees have multiple disabilities:
(**Please write in boxes**)

NUMBER OF EMPLOYEES

Q6. How many of your disabled employees have been in work for:
(**Please write in box**)

NUMBER OF EMPLOYEES

a. Less than 8 weeks

d. 8 week to less than 6 months

c. 6 months to less than 1 year

d. 1 years or more

**DISABILITY WORKING ALLOWANCE
AND SUPPORTED EMPLOYMENT AGENCIES**

**SCREENING QUESTIONNAIRE
FOR SUPPORTED EMPLOYMENT AGENCIES**

A STUDY BY THE INDEPENDENT POLICY STUDIES INSTITUTE
FOR THE DEPARTMENT OF SOCIAL SECURITY

Policy Studies Institute,
100 Park Village East,
LONDON NW1 3SR

Tel: 071 387 2171
Fax: 071 388 0914

Q7.   How many of your disabled employees currently work (per week):
       (Please write in box)

       NUMBER OF
       EMPLOYEES

       a.   Less than 16 hours

       d.   16 to 20 hours

       c.   20 to 30 hours

       d.   More than 30 hours

Q8.   How many of your disabled employees currently earn (per week):
       (Please write in box)

       NUMBER OF
       EMPLOYEES

       a.   Less than £50

       d.   £50 to less than £100

       c.   £100 to less than £150

       d.   More than £150

THANK YOU FOR COMPLETING THE QUESTIONNAIRE

99

COMPLETING THE QUESTIONNAIRE

Most questions asked you to give numbers or estimates, for example, the number of employees. If you cannot give an exact number, please give an estimate or your 'best guess'?

There is also an 'open-ended' questions. Again please write your response in the large boxes provided.

If you are unable to answer any of the questions, please write 'Don't know' next to the box provided.

All information given will be treated in the strictest confidence.

If you have any queries, please contact **GERRY ZARB** or **NIGEL JACKSON** at the address below:

Policy Studies Institute,
100 Park Village East,
London NW1 3SR

Tel: 071 387 2171
Fax: 071 388 0914

Q1a. How many disabled people are currently working in supported employment organised by your agency (including any disabled people working in supported employment within your own agency or in workshops managed by your agency)? **(Please write in box)**

TOTAL

b. How many of these are **male?** **(Please write in box)**

MALE

c. How many of these are **female?** **(Please write in box)**

FEMALE

Q2. What type, or types, of work are currently done by disabled people working in supported employment organised by your agency? **(Please write a brief description in box)**

Q3. How many of the disabled people currently working in supported employment organised by your agency are in each of the following age groups: **(Please write in box)**

NUMBER OF EMPLOYEES

a. 16 to 29

b. 30 to 39

c. 40 to 49

d. 50 and over

Q4. How many of the disabled people currently working in supported employment organised by your agency have: (**Please write in boxes**)

NUMBER OF EMPLOYEES

a. Learning difficulties/ mental handicaps/ nervous disorder

b. Mobility impairments including upper limb disorders relating to reaching, stretching, gripping or turning etc

c. Sensory impairments

d. Heart, respiratory & digestive problems

e. Head injuries

g. Others/miscellaneous

Q5. How many of the disabled people currently working in supported employment organised by your agency have multiple disabilities: (**Please write in box**)

NUMBER OF EMPLOYEES

Q6. How many of the disabled people currently working in supported employment organised by your agency have been in work for: (**Please write in box**)

NUMBER OF EMPLOYEES

a. Less than 8 weeks

d. 8 weeks to less than 6 months

c. 6 months to less than 1 year

d. 1 year or more

Q7. How many of the disabled people currently working in supported employment organised by your agency currently work (per week): (**Please write in box**)

NUMBER OF EMPLOYEES

a. Less than 16 hours

d. 16 to 20 hours

c. 20 to 30 hours

d. More than 30 hours

Q8. How many of the disabled people currently working in supported employment organised by your agency currently earn (per week): (**Please write in box**)

NUMBER OF EMPLOYEES

a. Less than £50

d. £50 to less than £100

c. £100 to less than £150

d. £150 and over

THANK YOU FOR COMPLETING THE QUESTIONNAIRE

IN CONFIDENCE

Reference No. < SPECIMEN>   (1-7)

Questionnaire for Disabled People Working in Supported Employment

COMPLETING THE QUESTIONNAIRE

The questions on this form are for the person named on the covering letter. If someone other than that person fills in the form, please make sure that all the questions are filled in from the named person's point of view.

Please answer the questions on the next 8 pages. Most questions can be answered:

by ticking a box, like this ....

or by writing in a number, like this .... `24`

Please ignore the little numbers beside the boxes; they just help us to record information.

The questionnaire asks for details of your current job, your take-home pay, the social security benefits that you are receiving, and about you and your household. No-one else will know what answers you give.

This information will help us to find out whether more disabled people might be entitled to a new social security benefit called the Disability Working Allowance.

If you have any questions, please contact **PHILIP TAYLOR** at the address below:

Policy Studies Institute
100 Park Village East
London NW1 3SR
Telephone 0171 - 468 0468
Fax 0171 - 388 0914

ABOUT YOUR PRESENT JOB

1   When did you start your present job?

Month ....   (8-9)

Year ....   (10-11)

2   Did you start you present job within the last 8 weeks?

Yes 1   (12)

No 2

3   How many hours (including regular overtime) do you usually work each week at the moment?

Please write the number of hours in this box ....   (13-14)

ABOUT YOUR USUAL TAKE-HOME PAY

4   What is your usual take-home pay at the moment?

By take-home pay, we mean the money you receive regularly after paying taxes and National Insurance.

Please write in the box the amount which you usually receive, including overtime payments, bonuses, tips, commission etc.

£ ☐   (15-18)

1

5 How often are you paid?

Weekly .... (19) [ ] 1

Fortnightly .... [ ] 2

Four weekly .... [ ] 3

Monthly .... [ ] 4

Other period (write in) .... [ ] 5

ABOUT YOUR BENEFITS

6 Which of the following benefits are you receiving at the moment?

Disability Living Allowance .... (20) [ ]

Attendance Allowance .... (21) [ ]

War Disablement Pension .... (22) [ ]

Industrial Injuries Disablement Benefit ... (23) [ ]

Invalid three wheeler from DSS .... (24) [ ]

Disability Working Allowance.................. (25) [ ] **Please skip to question 8**

IF YOU ARE NOT RECEIVING THE DISABILITY WORKING ALLOWANCE AT THE MOMENT

7 Have you ever received the Disability Working Allowance in the past? (26)

Yes .... [ ] 1

No .... [ ] 2

BEFORE YOU STARTED YOUR PRESENT JOB

8 Were you receiving any of the following benefits immediately before you started your present job?

Invalidity Benefit or Incapacity Benefit (27) [ ]

Severe Disablement Allowance........ (28) [ ]

Income Support .... (29) ⇨ [ ]

(34)
| Did this include a disability premium or higher pensioner premium for you? |
| Yes [ ] 1   No [ ] 2   Don't know [ ] 3 |

Council Tax Benefit .... (30) ⇨ [ ]

(35)
| Did this include a disability premium or higher pensioner premium for you? |
| Yes [ ] 1   No [ ] 2   Don't know [ ] 3 |

Housing Benefit .... (31) ⇨ [ ]

(36)
| Did this include a disability premium or higher pensioner premium for you? |
| Yes [ ] 1   No [ ] 2   Don't know [ ] 3 |

None of these benefits .... (32) [ ]

Don't know .... (33) [ ]

9 Were you working immediately before you started your present job?

(37)

Yes .... ☐ 1 **Please answer the next question.**

No .... ☐ 2 **Please skip to question 11**

IF YOU WERE WORKING IMMEDIATELY BEFORE YOU STARTED YOUR PRESENT JOB

10 How long had you been in a job immediately before you started this job?

(38)

Less than eight weeks .... ☐ 1

Eight weeks but less than three months .... ☐ 2

Three months but less than one year .... ☐ 3

One year but less than two years........................... ☐ 4

Two years or more .... ☐ 5

Now skip to question 12

IF YOU WERE NOT WORKING IMMEDIATELY BEFORE YOU STARTED YOUR PRESENT JOB

11 How long had you been out of work immediately before you started this job?

(39)

Less than eight weeks .... ☐ 1

Eight weeks but less than three months .... ☐ 2

Three months but less than one year .... ☐ 3

One year but less than two years........................... ☐ 4

Two years or more .... ☐ 5

4

ABOUT YOU AND YOUR HOUSEHOLD

12 How old are you?

(40-41)

Please write your age in this box .... ☐☐

13 Are you male or female?

(42)

Male .... ☐ 1

Female .... ☐ 2

14 Do you live with a partner, or your husband or wife at the moment?

(43)

Yes .... ☐ 1 **Please answer the next question**

No .... ☐ 2 **Please skip to question 19**

IF YOU ARE LIVING WITH YOUR HUSBAND, WIFE OR PARTNER AT THE MOMENT

15 Which of the following best describes what your husband, wife or partner is doing at present?(*Please tick only one box*)

(44)

Working in a paid job .... ☐ 1 **Please answer the next question**

Unemployed and looking for work .... ☐ 2 ⎤

On a training course or scheme .... ☐ 3 ⎟

Sick or disabled .... ☐ 4 ⎬ **Please skip to question 18**

Looking after home or family .... ☐ 5 ⎟

Retired .... ☐ 6 ⎟

Doing something else .... ☐ 7 ⎦

5

IF YOUR HUSBAND, WIFE OR PARTNER HAS A PAID JOB

16 What is your husband, wife or partner's take home pay *(after taxes and National Insurance)*?

Please write in the amount they usually receive, including regular overtime payments, bonuses, tips, commission etc.

£ [   ] (45-48)

17 How often are they paid? (49)

Weekly 1
Fortnightly 2
Four weekly 3
Monthly 4
Other period *(write in)* 5

IF YOUR HUSBAND, WIFE OR PARTNER IS NOT IN WORK AT THE MOMENT

18 Does your partner receive any of the following benefits at the moment?

Invalidity Benefit or Incapacity Benefit .... (50)
Severe Disablement Allowance .... (51)
Unemployment Benefit .... (52)
State/Retirement Pension .... (53)
Other benefits .... (54)
No benefits .... (55)
Don't know .... (56)

ABOUT YOUR SAVINGS

19 Do you and/or your husband, wife or partner have any personal savings?

(By savings we mean things like money in a bank or building society account, National Savings certificates, Premium Bonds, shares, unit trusts and other investments. Compensation for personal injury held in trust does not count as savings.)

(57)
Yes 1
No 2

IF YES: How much money do you have in savings?

(58)
No savings 1
£1 to £3,000 2
£3,001 to £8,000 3
£8,001 to £16,000 4
More than £16,000 5

ABOUT YOUR CHILDREN

20 Do you have any children?

(59)
Yes 1
No .... 2 **Please skip to question 22**

IF YOU HAVE ANY CHILDREN

21   Are any of your children living with you at the moment?

(60)

Yes .... ☐ 1

No .... ☐ 2

For each of your children living with you at the moment, please record their age and tick the box if they are also in full-time education

	Age	Full-time education
Oldest or only child	☐ (61-2)	☐ (73)
Next oldest child	☐ (63-4)	☐ (74)
Next oldest child...............	☐ (65-6)	☐ (75)
Next oldest child...............	☐ (67-8)	☐ (76)
Next oldest child...............	☐ (69-70)	☐ (77)
Next oldest child...............	☐ (71-2)	☐ (78)

22   Please can you tell us who filled in the questionnaire. Was it:

(79)

You (*the person in supported employment*) – without help .... ☐ 1

You (*the person in supported employment*) – with help .... ☐ 2

Someone else, for example, a relative, friend, assistant or carer ...... ☐ 3

Thank you very much for your help with this important research.

Remember that no-one at all, except the independent research staff who are carrying out the project, will see any of the information you give.

Please put this questionnaire into the stamped addressed envelope provided and post it off as soon as possible.

OTHER RESEARCH REPORTS AVAILABLE:

No.	Title	ISBN	Price
1.	Thirty Families: Their living standards in unemployment	0 11 761683 4	£6.65
2.	Disability, household income & expenditure	0 11 761755 5	£5.65
3.	Housing Benefit Reviews	0 11 761821 7	£16.50
4.	Social Security & Community Care: The case of the Invalid Care Allowance	0 11 761820 9	£9.70
5.	The Attendance Allowance Medical Examination: Monitoring consumer views	0 11 761819 5	£5.50
6.	Lone Parent Families in the UK	0 11 761868 3	£12.75
7.	Incomes In and Out of Work	0 11 761910 8	£17.20
8.	Working the Social Fund	0 11 761952 3	£9.00
9.	Evaluating the Social Fund	0 11 761953 1	£22.00
10.	Benefits Agency National Customer Survey 1991	0 11 761956 6	£16.00
11.	Customer Perceptions of Resettlement Units	0 11 761976 6	£13.75
12.	Survey of Admissions to London Resettlement Units	0 11 761977 9	£8.00
13.	Researching the Disability Working Allowance Self Assessment Form	0 11 761834 9	£7.25
14.	Child Support Unit National Client Survey 1992	0 11 762060 2	£30.00
15.	Preparing for Council Tax Benefit	0 11 762061 0	£5.65
16.	Contributions Agency Customer Satisfaction Survey 1992	0 11 762064 5	£18.00
17.	Employers' Choice of Pension Schemes: report of a qualitative study	0 11 762073 4	£5.00
18.	GPs and IVB: A qualitative study of the role of GPs in the award of Invalidity Benefit	0 11 762077 7	£12.00
19.	Invalidity Benefit: A Survey of Recipients	0 11 762087 4	£10.75

43. Paying for Rented Housing 0 11 762370 9 £19.00

44. Resettlement Agency Customer Satisfaction Survey 1994 0 11 762371 7 £16.00

45. Changing Lives and the Role of Income Support 0 11 762405 5 £20.00

46. Social Assistance in OECD Countries: Synthesis Report 0 11 762407 1 £22.00

47. Social Assistance in OECD Countries: Country Report 0 11 762408 X £47.00

48. Leaving Family Credit 0 11 762411 X £18.00

49. Women and Pensions 0 11 762422 5 £35.00

50. Pensions and Divorce 0 11 762423 5 £25.00

51. Child Support Agency Client Satisfaction Survey 1995 0 11 762424 1 £22.00

52. Take Up of Second Adult Rebate 0 11 762390 3 £17.00

53. Moving off Income Support 0 11 762394 6 £26.00

55. Housing Benefit and Service Charges 0 11 762399 7 £25.00

Social Security Research Yearbook 1990–91 0 11 761747 4 £8.00

Social Security Research Yearbook 1991–92 0 11 761833 0 £12.00

Social Security Research Yearbook 1992–93 0 11 762150 1 £13.75

Social Security Research Yearbook 1993–94 0 11 762302 4 £16.50

Social Security Research Yearbook 1994–95 0 11 762362 8 £20.00

109

Further information regarding the content of the above may be obtained from:

Department of Social Security
Attn. Keith Watson
Social Research Branch
Analytical Services Division 5
10th Floor, Adelphi
1–11 John Adam Street
London WC2N 6HT
Telephone: 0171 962 8557

Printed in the UK for The Stationery Office
Dd303169 11/96 C11 G3397 10170

The Stationery Office

Published by The Stationery Office and available from:

The Stationery Office Publications Centre
(mail, telephone and fax orders only)
PO Box 276, London SW8 5DT
General enquiries 0171 873 0011
Telephone orders 0171 873 9090
Fax orders 0171 873 8200

The Stationery Office Bookshops
49 High Holborn, London WC1V 6HB
(counter service and fax orders only)
Fax 0171 831 1326
68-69 Bull Street, Birmingham B4 6AD
0121 236 9696 Fax 0121 236 9699
33 Wine Street, Bristol BS1 2BQ
0117 926 4306 Fax 0117 929 4515
9-21 Princess Street, Manchester M60 8AS
0161 834 7201 Fax 0161 833 0634
16 Arthur Street, Belfast BT1 4GD
01232 238451 Fax 01232 235401
71 Lothian Road, Edinburgh EH3 9AZ
0131 479 3141 Fax 0131 479 3142
The Stationery Office Oriel Bookshop
The Friary, Cardiff CF1 4AA
01222 395548 Fax 01222 384347

The Stationery Office's Accredited Agents
(see Yellow Pages)

and through good booksellers